सीताराम

Rama Raksha Stotra
&
Rama Jayam - Likhita Japam Mala

:

Journal for Writing the Rama-Nama
100,000 Times alongside the Sacred Hindu Text
Rama Raksha Stotra,
with English Translation & Transliteration

::

श्रीरामरक्षा-स्तोत्रं
व
राम जयम - लिखित जपम
राम-नाम लेखन माला

(एक लाख राम-नाम लेखन हेतु)

Belongs to ______________________________

Published by: **Rama-Nama Journals**
(an Imprint of e1i1 Corporation)

Title: **Rama Raksha Stotra & Rama Jayam - Likhita Japam Mala**
Sub-Title: **Journal for Writing the Rama-Nama 100,000 Times alongside the Sacred Hindu Text Rama Raksha Stotra, with English Translation & Transliteration**

Author: **Sushma**

Parts of this book have been derived/inspired from our other publication:
"Rama Hymns" (Authored by Sushma)

Identifiers

ISBN: **978-1-945739-18-7** (Paperback)

—o—

www.**e1i1**.com -- www.**OnlyRama**.com
email: **e1i1***books***e1i1**@gmail.com

Our books can be bought online, or at Amazon, or any bookstore. If a book is not available at your neighborhood bookstore they will be happy to order it for you. (Certain Hardcover Editions may not be immediately available—we apologize)

Some of our Current/Forthcoming Books are listed below. Please note that this is a partial list and that we are continually adding new books. Please visit www.**e1i1**.com / www.**onlyRama**.com for current offerings.

- **Tulsi Ramayana—The Hindu Bible:** Ramcharitmanas with English Translation & Transliteration
- **Tulsi-Ramayana Rama-Nama Mala (multiple volumes):** Legacy Journals for Writing the Rama Name alongside Tulsidas Ramcharitmanas—contains English Translation & Transliteration, Inspirational Quotes of Hindu saints, and space for you to jot down your spiritual sentiments on a daily basis. Once embellished with your Rama-Namas, these books become priceless treasures which you can present to your loved ones—a true gift of love, labor, caring, wishing, and above all—Devotion.
- **Ramcharitmanas:** Ramayana of Tulsidas with Transliteration (in English)
- **Ramayana, Large**: Tulsi Ramcharitmanas, Hindi only Edition, Large Font and Paper size
- **Ramayana, Medium**: Tulsi Ramcharitmanas, Hindi only Edition, Medium Font and Paper size
- **Ramayana, Small**: Tulsi Ramcharitmanas, Hindi only Edition, Small Font and Paper size
- **Sundarakanda:** The Fifth-Ascent of Tulsi Ramayana
- **RAMA GOD:** In the Beginning - Upanishad Vidya (Know Thyself)
- **Purling Shadows:** And A Dream Called Life - Upanishad Vidya (Know Thyself)
- **Fiery Circle:** Upanishad Vidya (Know Thyself)
- **Rama Hymns:** Hanuman-Chalisa, Rama-Raksha-Stotra, Bhushumdi-Ramayana, Nama-Ramayanam, Rama-Shata-Nama-Stotra, etc. with Transliteration & English Translation
- **Rama Jayam - Likhita Japam Mala alongside Sacred Hindu Texts (several):** Journals for Writing the Rama Name 100,000 Times alongside various Hindu Texts, with English Translation & Transliteration. Embellish these Books with your Rama-Namas and they become transformed into priceless treasures which you can later gift to your loved ones.
- **Rama Jayam - Likhita Japam Mala alongside Rama-Mantras (several):** Journals for Writing the Rama Name 100,000 Times alongside the Rama-Mantras from one lettered to thirty-two others. Embellish these with your Rama-Namas and they become transformed into priceless treasures.

-- On our website may be found links to renditions of Rama Hymns –

-- Rama Mantras/Hymns/Pictures are also available printed on Quality Shirts from Amazon. See our website for details --

rāma-nāma mahimā

In this modern era—which is awash with the six *Gunas* of Māyā: *Kāma* (Lust), *Krodha* (Anger), *Lobha* (Greed), *Moha* (Infatuation), *Mada* (Pride) & *Mātsarya* (Envy)—we find our minds sinking in worldliness. It seems that despite their best intent, no one can remain unsullied from the taints of Kali; this appears to be the fait-accompli of the *Kali-Yuga*—a very sad fate indeed. But despair not, because there is hope—we find ourselves assured.

The Japa of Rāma-Nāma (Rāma-Name) is the supreme path to salvation in this *Kali-Yuga*, assure our Scriptures; there is no Dharma higher than Nāma-Dharma in this Age of Kali—we are told. Sing the praises of the Lord and remain engaged in *Nāma-Smarana*—is the advice given to us by our saints. The chanting of Rāma-Nāma is The-One-Supreme-Path to escape the clutches of *Kali-Yuga*—declares Rāmacharitmānas—and in fact it **is the one and only Dharma which is easy and feasible in the present times.**

Many of the Hindu saints zealously assert: "In this Kali-Yuga, there is no other means, no other means, no other means of salvation—other than chanting the holy name Rāma, chanting the holy name Rāma, chanting the holy name Rāma."

Rāma-Japa—the constant repetition of the **Supreme-Mantra 'Rāma'**—is usually done mentally, or on a rosary; but there is one extremely efficacious method of this Japa: the *Likhita-Japa*, or the Written-Chant.

The practice of writing the Rāma Mantra over and over on paper is called the *Likhita-Japa*. This written form of Japa is a lasting record of your chant, remaining ever imbued with those holy vibrations, for all times, for the benefit of you and the future generations.

In India, as you may know, devotees of God have been chanting the name 'Rāma' and writing the Name 'Rāma'—pages upon pages of it, running into billions and billions, for ages. Hindu children are taught to write the Rāma-Nāma from their very childhood, and the writing competitions of the One *Lakh* Rāma–Nāma, brings up nostalgic memories for many Hindus.

The completed Rāma-Nāma books are variously utilized. Some devotees preserve them carefully for their holy association and divine energy, while others donate them to temples. The written Rāma-Nāma Books are used in the foundations of temples during construction; they add divine energy to the Temples—while in turn strengthening the foundations of the spiritual life of those who wrote the Rāma Name. Also some collected Rāma-Nama books are placed in crypts to be used during *Yagna's* in Rāma Temples; and temples preserve these books for future. Devotees also place their own written Rāma-Nāma Books during the laying of foundation of their new homes, or in their *Pooja*-Room.

Of those of our Chakras (psychic centers), where our *Sanchit* (accumulated) Karmas are stored, Rāma is the *Beej Mantra*. The writing of Rāma-Nāma helps cleanse the Chakras, and our suppressed emotions, and the negative *Sanskaras* of the subconscious, and our remnant/unworked Karmas from past lives—which all get purged through the repetition of the Rāma-Nāma Mantra.

The chanting of Rāma-Nāma is a direct way to liberation. As per belief, devotees attempt to write down at least Eighty-Four Lakh (84,00,000) Rāma-Nāmas to get out of the birth-death cycle of Eighty-Four Lakh *Yonīs*, and thereby attain to salvation.

The *Likhita* Rāma-Nāma Japa is a powerful and transformative tool. As you write the Rāma-Nāma, all the senses become engaged in the service of Lord-God, and you find yourself simultaneously chanting and hearing and contemplating on the Lord—everything comes together naturally. This method clears away your thoughts and helps concentrate the entirety of your soul upon the Divine.

Any Japa is beneficial but somehow writing the Rāma-Nāma on paper brings up a great singularity of focus within the mind—and the peace of heart which ensues is something which is not so easily achieved with other forms of Japa. The written form of Rāma-Japa is somehow able to engage those parts of our body-mind continuum which other methods can not—and our meditative stance is able to achieve much deeper levels.

There is something special which will happen when you write the Rāma-Nāma—as you will discover. Peace and tranquility will surround you as you write the Supreme-Mantra: Rāma. The Rāma-Nāma will impart to you supreme strength, and great tolerance to withstand the vicissitudes of life. Bright unclouded wisdom will illumine your mind. You will find yourself in complete sense of surrender to your inner being. The resonance of God will resonate throughout your mind-body continuity. You will feel a flux of divine energy resonating within you. You will get great power and peace in your everyday life. The chanting of Rāma Mantra will protect your inner world as well as the outside.

Although the Rāma-Mantra is the gateway to higher consciousness and spiritual upliftment, but even at such junctures—when you find yourself in odd situations, where all the paths seem blocked—then just walking away from everything and simply writing the Rāma Nāma, will give you much needed clarity of thought—and a divine inspiration that will show the way out.

Thus, the Rāma Nāma is very transformative: with it you gain a balanced progress in your outside world and the inner. *Sant* Tulsidās says in *Rāmacharitmānas*: Place the Rāma-Nāma Jewel at the threshold, and there will be light both inside and out; i.e. a constant chant of the Rāma-Nāma from the mouth—the doorway to the body—will bring you external materialistic wellbeing, and also an inner spiritual wellness—both. Incredibly, with the Rāma-Nāma, you get to have the best of both the worlds.

According to the Vedas, just as the sun dispels the darkness, the chanting of Rāma-Nāma dispels all the evils and obstacles of life. The Rāma Nāma cures agony and showers the blessings of God; all righteous wishes get fulfilled; jealousy and pride disappear; life becomes imbued with satisfaction and peace; all of life's needs fall in place automatically—just like a miracle of nature guiding nature's forces. You may not always get what you want in the exact same form, but the Rāma-Nāma will purify things and bring to you the same needed happiness and bliss in a much more refined and lasting way. Your life will truly become filled with tranquility. Thus, with the Rāma-Nāma, an immense sense of spiritual wellbeing is experienced apart from gain of material happiness.

For *Likhita* Japa, you can write the Rāma-Nāma in any language of your choice—after all, Name is the connecting chord between the Divine and your inner self—but writing the Rāma-Nāma in its original Sanskrit form is simply superlative—most excellent, most effective. Sanskrit is *Deva-Bhāshā* (the language-of-gods). If you do not know how to write **राम** in Sanskrit it is quite easy. In the figure below, trace the contours 1-2 (which is the sound of underlined letters in the word '**ru**n'), 3-4 (the sound of underlined letter a in 'ark'), 5-6 & 7-8 (the underlined mu in '**mu**st') and lastly the line 9-10; and that's it. Note the similarity of English **R** , **M** to the Sanskrit **र** , **म** , (and English words used here like *Name, Saint*—similar to the Sanskrit *Nāma, Sant.*) All European languages have their roots in Sanskrit, the great grand mother tongue of most.

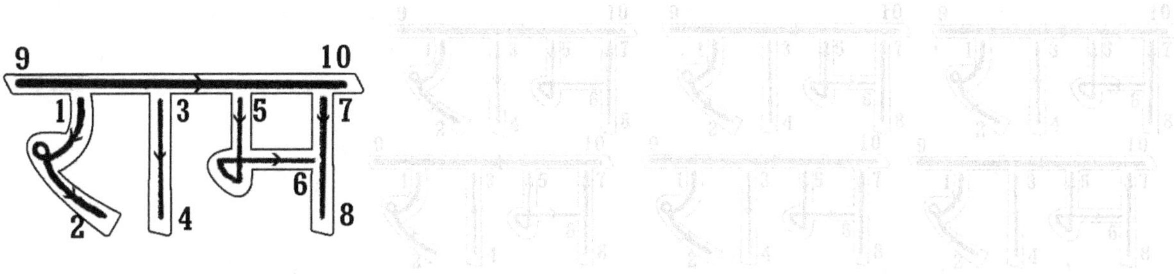

Write the Supreme-Mantra Rāma with reverence, every day, preferably at a set time, or as and when possible, in small measures, or copiously—howsoever your situation permits. There are no hard rules, do what feels good to your Soul. The important thing is to engage in the *Likhita*-Japa. When completed, you could keep the books in your Worship-Room, preserve them as treasures to pass on to future generations, donate them to Rāma Temples, or gift them to your loved ones—who will thereby inculcate crucial values from you, and learn the importance of the Rāma-Nāma, and get inspired with Hindu Values, especially so the younger ones.

While writing, focus your mind on the Rāma-Name and chant it within. Imagine Sītā-Rāma showering you with their bliss. Try to stay free of distractions, and with time you will find that your mind will take a natural meditative stance while engaged in the written Rāma-Nāma Japa.

You can choose any notebook or paper to write on, not necessarily this one. Traditionally people will write the Rāma Name in red ink on straight lines; but some devotees will also simultaneously make an interesting design—by changing the orientation of lines, or using different colors, utilizing an underlying outline to base their Japa upon. Do what comes naturally; no hard rules.

Find a set of pencils or pens which write and feel beautiful to you. If making an intricate pattern use pens that have finer points—but see that the ink does not bleed through to the other side.

Ideally, you will have a special set of pens kept purely for the Likhita Japa. This will make it easier for you to enter into the spirit of things. You will find that such implements—which you habitually use for holy tasks—build up energy and holy resonance.

A grid of 21 by 48 (1008 boxes) is provided for you as a guide—to be able to write a thousand Rāma Names per page. Some people will ignore the boxes and write in their own style, as and how their own inspiration leads them, creating their own design on the pages; and sometimes the design will preclude using all the boxes; but still, with 108 pages to write upon, and with space for 1008 names per page, you should be able to cross the 100,000 Rāma-Nāma objective of the book. The 100,000 target is merely suggestive—it assumes you write one Rāma-Nāma per box; obviously your mileage will vary, and you will get a figure more or less than 100,000, depending upon if you write smaller or larger. If need be, please utilize the empty spaces on the pages.

The pages contain the śrī-rāma-rakṣā-stotra Text (Hymn for gaining Shri Rama's Protection) as font outlines. Before beginning your Likhita Japa for that page, if you can write within the stotraṁ outlines the Rāma-Nāmas—using color/size/slant which is different from the outside—then it will make those Verses stand out. Or if you cannot write so tiny, then simply color the verses using colored pencil or highlighter—that way the Text will pop out from amongst the waves of surrounding Rāma-Nāmas. We wish you Happy Rāma-Nāma Japa.

Once embellished with your Rāma-Nāmas, this śrī-rāma-rakṣā-stotra book will become a priceless treasure which you can present to your loved ones—an unparalleled gift of love, labor, caring, wishing, and above all—Devotion.

—o—o—o—o—o—o—o—o—o—o—o—

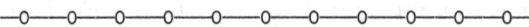

राम राम

राम
राम
राम
राम
राम
राम
राम
राम
राम
राम
राम
राम
राम
राम
राम
राम
राम
राम
राम
राम
राम
राम
राम
राम
राम
राम
राम
राम
राम
राम
राम
राम
राम
राम
राम
राम
राम
राम
राम
राम
राम
राम
राम
राम
राम
राम
राम
राम

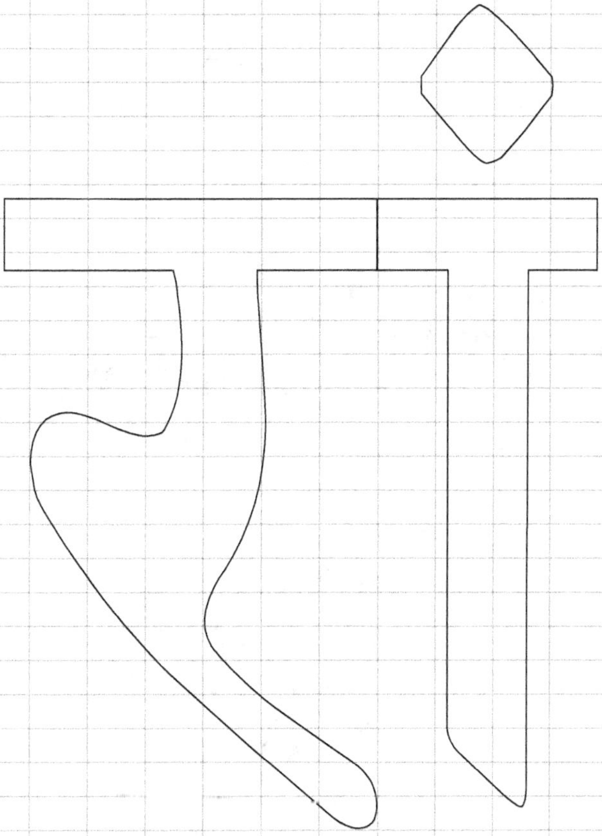

Today's Date : ______________

राम राम

राम
राम
राम
राम
राम
राम
राम
राम
राम
राम
राम
राम
राम
राम
राम
राम
राम
राम
राम
राम
राम
राम
राम
राम
राम
राम
राम
राम
राम
राम
राम
राम
राम
राम
राम
राम
राम
राम
राम
राम
राम
राम
राम
राम
राम
राम
राम
राम

अथ
श्री रामरक्षा
स्तोत्रं

॥ अथ श्रीरामरक्षा स्तोत्रं ॥

॥ atha śrī rāma rakṣā stotraṁ ॥

_______________:*Today's Date*

राम राम

atha śrī rāma rakṣā stotraṁ

(Now commences śrī-rāma-rakṣā stotraṁ)

Today's Date : ________________

राम राम

राम राम

अस्य
श्रीरामरक्षास्तोत्र
मन्त्रस्य बुधकौशिक
ऋषिः

asya śrī rāma rakṣāstotra mantrasya budha kauśika ṛṣiḥ

अस्य श्रीरामरक्षास्तोत्रमन्त्रस्य बुधकौशिक ऋषिः

asya śrī rāma rakṣāstotra mantrasya budha kauśika ṛṣiḥ

श्रीसीतारामचन्द्रो देवता अनुष्टुप् छन्दः

śrī sītā rāma candro devatā anuṣṭup chandaḥ

______________:Today's Date

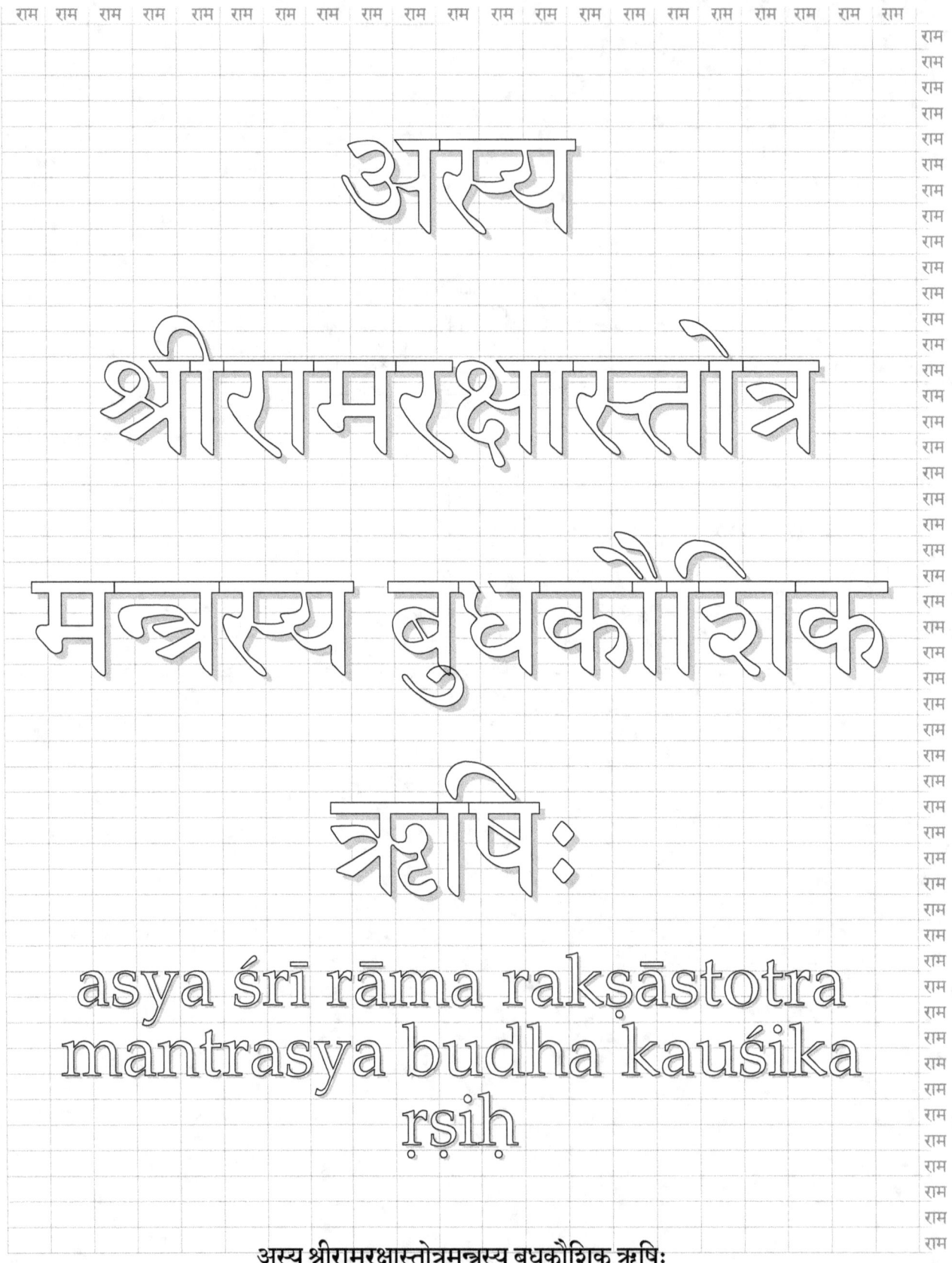

राम राम

राम राम

श्रीसीतारामचन्द्रो देवता अनुष्टुप् छन्दः

śrī sītā rāma candro devatā anuṣṭup chandaḥ

Of this Rāmrakshāstotra (**Hymn-of-Rāma**—for gaining **Protection**) the *Rishi* is: Buddha-Kaushik; the eight syllable quarter *Anushthap* is: the Meter; and the Deity: **Shrī Sītā-Ramachandra**.

Today's Date : ________________

राम राम

राम राम

सीता शक्तिः श्रीमान् हनुमान् कीलकं

sītā śaktiḥ śrīmān hanumān kīlakaṁ

सीता शक्तिः श्रीमान् हनुमान् कीलकं

sītā śaktiḥ śrīmān hanumān kīlakaṁ

श्रीरामचन्द्रप्रीत्यर्थे रामरक्षास्तोत्रजपे विनियोगः ॥

śrī rāma candra prītyarthe rāma rakṣā stotra jape viniyogaḥ .

______________ :Today's Date

राम राम

राम राम

श्रीरामचन्द्रप्रीत्यर्थे
रामरक्षास्तोत्रजपे
विनियोगः ॥

śrī rāma candra prītyarthe
rāma rakṣā stotra jape
viniyogaḥ .

Shrī Sītā is the underlying energy: *Shakti*; and **Shrī Hanumān**: the anchor; the usage is: Recitation. This Rāmrakshāstotra is invoked through recitation—to please Shrī Ramachandra and earn His benediction and grace.

Today's Date: ____________

राम राम

राम राम

ध्यायेदाजानुबाहुं

धृतशरधनुषं

बद्धपद्मासनस्थं

dhyāye dājānu bāhuṁ dhṛta
śara dhanuṣaṁ baddha
padmā sanasthaṁ

-- *अथ ध्यानम्* . *atha dhyānam* --

ध्यायेदाजानुबाहुं धृतशरधनुषं बद्धपद्मासनस्थं

dhyāye dājānu bāhuṁ dhṛta śara dhanuṣaṁ baddha padmā sanasthaṁ

पीतं वासो वसानं नवकमलदलस्पर्धिनेत्रं प्रसन्नम् ।

pītaṁ vāso vasānaṁ nava kamala dala spardhi netraṁ prasannam ,

__________________ :*Today's Date*

पीतं वासो वसानं

नवकमलदलस्पर्धि

नेत्रं प्रसन्नम् ।

pītaṁ vāso vasānaṁ nava
kamala dala spardhi netraṁ
prasannam ,

-- [**Meditate**] --

Meditate upon Him: of abundant arms, holding bow and arrows in His hands, donning yellow apparels, seated in a lotus posture; of a beaming countenance, whose exquisite eyes—which compete with the petals of fresh lotus

राम राम

राम राम

वामाङ्करूढसीतामुख
कमलमिलल्लोचनं
नीरदाभं

vāmāṅka rūḍha sītā mukha kamala mila llocanaṁ nīra dābhaṁ

वामाङ्करूढसीतामुखकमलमिलल्लोचनं नीरदाभं

vāmāṅka rūḍha sītā mukha kamala mila llocanaṁ nīra dābhaṁ

नानालंकारदीप्तं दधतमुरुजटामण्डलं रामचन्द्रम् ॥

nānā laṁkāra dīptaṁ dadhata murujaṭā maṇḍalaṁ rāma candram .

-- *इति ध्यानम्* . *iti dhyānam* --

________________ :*Today's Date*

राम राम

नानालंकारदीप्तं

दधतमुरुजटामण्डलं

रामचन्द्रम् ॥

nānā laṁkāra dīptaṁ

dadhata murujaṭā maṇḍalaṁ

rāma candram .

—are locked on the lovely lotus-faced Sītā sitting to his left. Upon Him—of a hue dark as heavy rain-clouds, crowned with long dense matted hair, who shines resplendent with several ornaments—upon Him, Bhagwan Shrī Ramachandra, meditate.

-- [Meditation concludes (Mantras Begin)] --

Today's Date : ____________

राम राम

राम राम

चरितं रघुनाथस्य

शतकोटि

प्रविस्तरम् ।

caritaṁ raghu nāthasya śata
koṭi pravis taram ,

चरितं रघुनाथस्य शतकोटि प्रविस्तरम् ।

caritaṁ raghu nāthasya śata koṭi pravis taram ,

एकैकमक्षरं पुंसां महापातकनाशनम् ॥ १ ॥

ek aikam akṣaraṁ puṁsāṁ mahā pātaka nāśa nam . 1 .

________________ Today's Date

राम राम

राम राम

एकैकमक्षरं पुंसां
महापातकनाशनम्
॥ १ ॥

ek aikam akṣaraṁ puṁsāṁ
mahā pātaka nāśa nam . 1 .

Illimitable the resplendent glory of Raghunāth, a hundred billion words in extent—each and every word of which destructs the most grievous sin.

राम राम

ध्यात्वा

नीलोत्पलश्यामं

रामं

राजीवलोचनम् ।

dhyātvā nīlotpala śyāmaṁ
rāmaṁ rājīva locanam ,

राम राम

ध्यात्वा नीलोत्पलश्यामं रामं राजीवलोचनम् ।

dhyā tvā nīl otpala śyāmaṁ rāmaṁ rājīva locanam ,

जानकीलक्ष्मणोपेतं जटामुकुटमण्डितम् ॥ २ ॥

jānakī lakṣmaṇo petaṁ jaṭā mukuṭa maṇḍitam . 2 .

_________________ :Today's Date

जानकीलक्ष्मणोपेतं
जटामुकुटमण्डितम्

॥ २ ॥

jānakī lakṣmaṇo petaṁ jaṭā
mukuṭa maṇḍitam . 2 .

Meditating upon Him—of a hue that is a dark blue, with eyes like a pair of lotuses, well-adorned with a crown of matted hair—accompanied by Sītā and Lakshman;

राम राम

राम राम

सासितूण
धनुर्बाणपाणिं
नक्तंचरान्तकम् ।

sāsitūṇa dhanur bāṇa pāṇiṁ
naktaṁ carāntakam ,

सासितूणधनुर्बाणपाणिं नक्तंचरान्तकम् ।
sāsitūṇa dhanur bāṇa pāṇiṁ naktaṁ carāntakam ,
स्वलीलया जगत्त्रातुमविर्भूतमजं विभुम् ॥ ३ ॥
sva līlayā jagat trātuma virbhūta majaṁ vibhum . 3 .

________________ :Today's Date

राम राम

राम राम

स्वलीलया

जगत्त्रातुम

विर्भूतमजं

विभुम् ॥ ३ ॥

sva līlayā jagat trātuma
virbhūta majaṁ vibhum . 3 .

who wields sword, bow and arrows, the destroyer of demons; who, though birthless, of his own will became Incarnate to protect the world—

Today's Date : ______________

राम राम

रामरक्षां पठेत्प्राज्ञः

पापघ्नीं

सर्वकामदाम् ।

rāma rakṣāṁ paṭhet prājñaḥ pāpaghnīṁ sarva kāma dām

,

रामरक्षां पठेत्प्राज्ञः पापघ्नीं सर्वकामदाम् ।

rāma rakṣāṁ paṭhet prājñaḥ pāpa ghnīṁ sarva kāma dām ,

शिरो मे राघवः पातु भालं दशरथात्मजः ॥ ४ ॥

śiro me rāghavaḥ pātu bhālaṁ daśarath ātmajaḥ . 4 .

_______________ Today's Date

शिरो मे राघवः पातु
भालं दशरथात्मजः
॥ ४ ॥

śiro me rāghavaḥ pātu
bhālaṁ daśarath ātmajaḥ
. 4 .

—meditating upon Him: Shrī Rāma, the wise recite this Rāmrakshāstotra—which destroys all sins, grants every desire, and bestows God's protection. Now then I pray: May Rāghav guard the head; may Dasharatha's son protect the forehead.

Today's Date : ____________

राम राम

राम राम

कौसल्येयो दृशौ पातु विश्वामित्रप्रियः श्रुती ।

kausalyeyo dṛśau pātu viśvā mitra priyaḥ śrutī ,

कौसल्येयो दृशौ पातु विश्वामित्रप्रियः श्रुती ।

kausal yeyo dṛśau pātu viśvā mitra priyaḥ śrutī ,

घ्राणं पातु मखत्राता मुखं सौमित्रिवत्सलः ॥ ५ ॥

ghrāṇaṁ pātu makha trātā mukhaṁ saumitri vatsalaḥ . 5 .

______________ :Today's Date

राम राम

घ्राणं पातु मखत्राता

मुखं

सौमित्रिवत्सलः

॥ ५ ॥

ghrāṇaṁ pātu makhatrātā
mukhaṁ saumitri vatsalaḥ
. 5 .

May the eyes stand protected by the son of Kausalyā; the ears by the favorite disciple of Vishwāmitra; the nasals by the savior of sacrificial fires; the mouth by Him who is most affectionate to the son of Sumitrā.

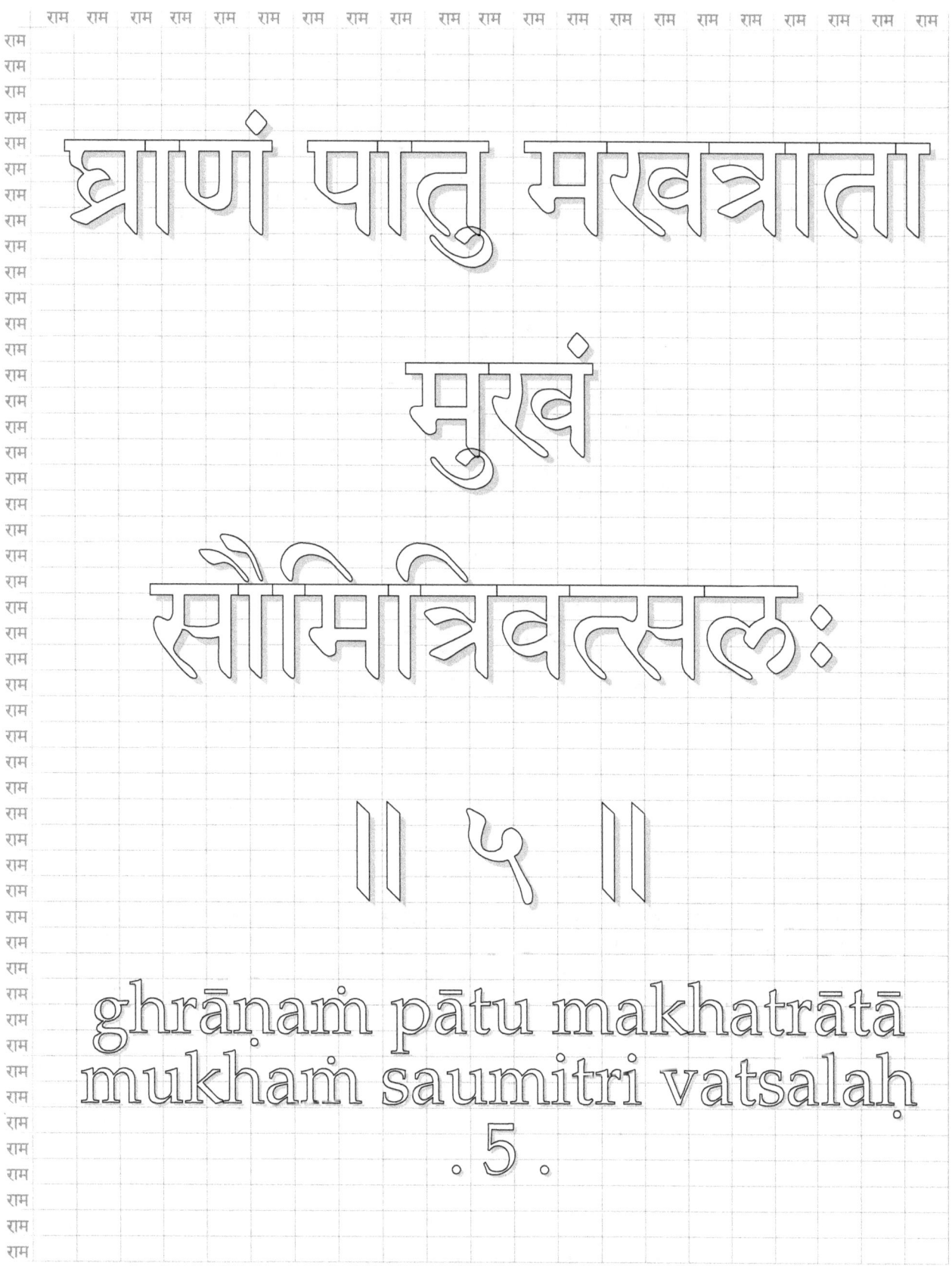

राम राम

राम राम

जिह्वां विद्यानिधिः

पातु कण्ठं

भरतवंदितः ।

jihvāṁ vidyā nidhiḥ pātu
kaṇṭhaṁ bharata vaṁditaḥ ,

जिह्वां विद्यानिधिः पातु कण्ठं भरतवंदितः ।
jihvāṁ vidyā nidhiḥ pātu kaṇṭhaṁ bharata vaṁditaḥ ,

स्कन्धौ दिव्यायुधः पातु भुजौ भग्नेशकार्मुकः ॥ ६ ॥

skandhau divyā yudhaḥ pātu bhujau bhag neśa kārmukaḥ . 6 .

_______________ :Today's Date

राम राम

स्कन्धौ दिव्यायुधः

पातु भुजौ

भग्नेशकार्मुकः

॥ ६ ॥

skandhau divyāyudhaḥ pātu
bhujau bhagneśa kārmukaḥ
. 6 .

May the ocean-of-wisdom protect the tongue; Bharat's Lord the neck. May the wielder of celestial weapons shield the shoulders; may the arms be fortified by His mighty arms who effortlessly broke the Bow of Shankara.

Today's Date : ____________________

राम राम

करौ सीतापतिः पातु

हृदयं जामदग्न्यजित्

।

karau sītā patiḥ pātu
hṛdayaṁ jāma dagnya jit ,

करौ सीतापतिः पातु हृदयं जामदग्न्यजित् ।

karau sītā patiḥ pātu hṛdayaṁ jāma dagnya jit ,

मध्यं पातु खरध्वंसी नाभिं जाम्बवदाश्रयः ॥ ७ ॥

madhyaṁ pātu khara dhvaṁsī nābhiṁ jāmbavad āśrayaḥ . 7 .

________________ :Today's Date

राम राम

राम राम

मध्यं पातु खरध्वंसी

नाभिं जाम्बवदाश्रयः

॥ ७ ॥

madhyaṁ pātu khara dhvaṁsī nābhiṁ jāmbavad āśrayaḥ . 7 .

May the Lord of Sītā protect the hands; may He, who won over Parshurām, protect the heart; may the middle be preserved by the slayer of demon Khara; may He, who gave shelter to Jāmvant, shelter the navel.

Today's Date : ____________

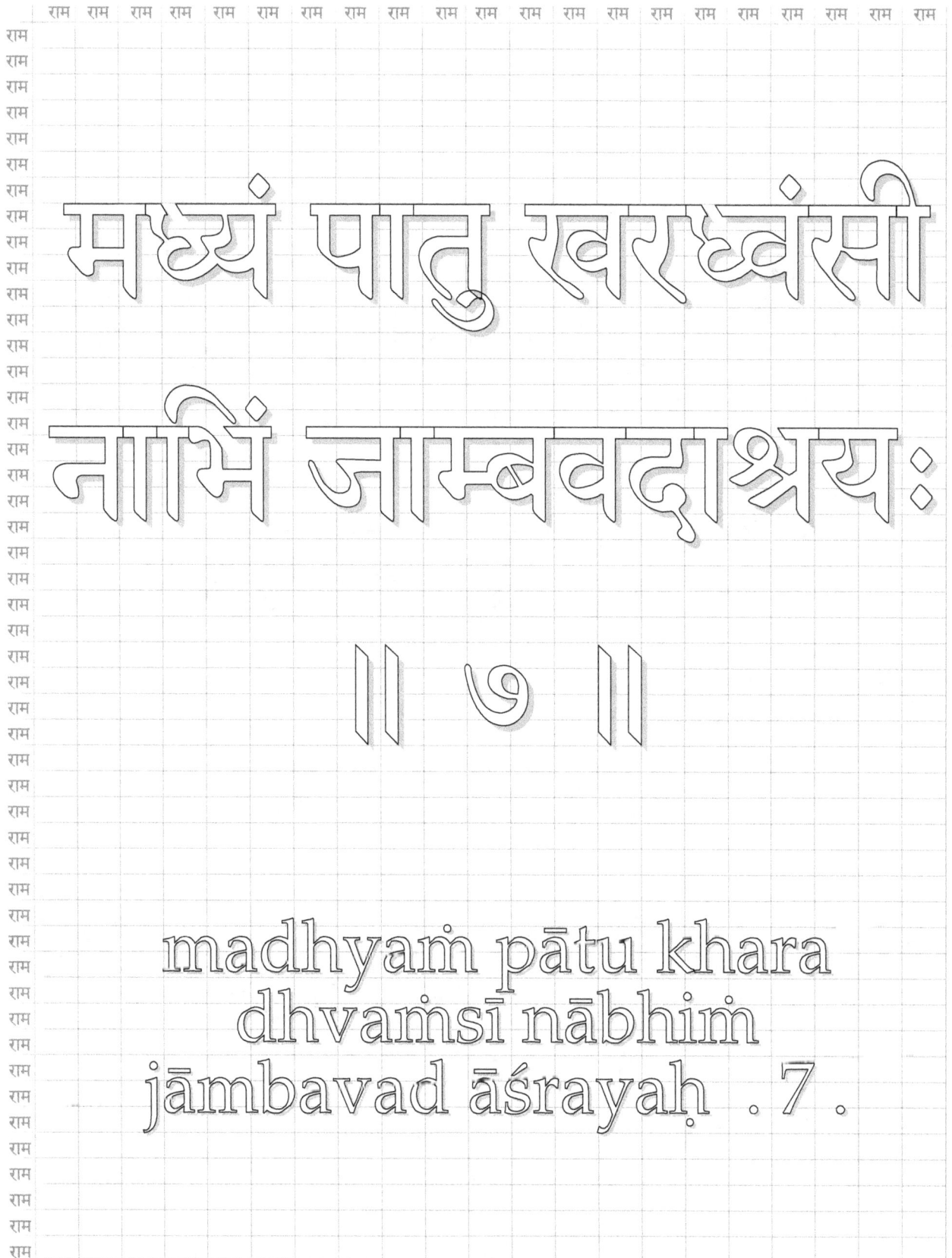

राम राम

सुग्रीवेशः कटी पातु
सक्थिनी हनुमत्प्रभुः

।

sugrīveśaḥ kaṭī pātu sakthinī
hanumat prabhuḥ ,

राम राम

सुग्रीवेशः कटी पातु सक्थिनी हनुमत्प्रभुः ।
sugrī veśaḥ kaṭī pātu sakthinī hanumat prabhuḥ ,
ऊरू रघूत्तमः पातु रक्षःकुलविनाशकृत् ॥ ८ ॥
ūrū raghū ttamaḥ pātu rakṣaḥ kula vināśakṛt . 8 .

______________:Today's Date

ऊरू रघूत्तमः पातु
रक्षःकुलविनाशकृत्

॥ ८ ॥

ūrū raghūttamaḥ pātu
rakṣaḥ kula vināśakṛt . 8 .

May the Master of Sugrīva protects the waist; may the Lord of Hanumān protect the hips. May the laps stand protected by the best of Raghus scion—who is the destroyer of lineage of demons.

Today's Date : ______________

राम राम

राम राम

जानुनी सेतुकृत्पातु जङ्घे दशमुखान्तकः ।

jānunī setu kṛtpātu jaṅaghe daśa mukhāntakaḥ ,

जानुनी सेतुकृत्पातु जङ्घे दशमुखान्तकः ।

jānunī setu kṛtpātu jaṅaghe daśa mukh āntakaḥ ,

पादौ बिभीषणश्रीदः पातु रामोऽखिलं वपुः ॥ ९ ॥

pādau bibhīṣaṇ aśrīdaḥ pātu rām o'khilaṁ vapuḥ . 9 .

_______________ :Today's Date

राम राम

पादौ बिभीषणश्रीदः

पातु रामोऽखिलं

वपुः ॥ ९ ॥

pādau bibhīṣaṇaśrīdaḥ pātu

rāmo'khilaṁ vapuḥ . 9 .

May He, who spanned a bridge across the sea—guard the knees; may the slayer of the Ten-Headed demon—protect the shins; may the bestower of kingdom to Vibhīshan—protect the feet. May Shrī Rāma be the armor of the entire body.

राम राम

राम राम

एतां रामबलोपेतां

रक्षां यः सुकृती

पठेत् ।

etāṁ rāmabalo petāṁ
rakṣāṁ yaḥ sukṛtī paṭhet ,

एतां रामबलोपेतां रक्षां यः सुकृती पठेत् ।
etāṁ rāma balo petāṁ rakṣāṁ yaḥ sukṛtī paṭhet ,
स चिरायुः सुखी पुत्री विजयी विनयी भवेत् ॥ १० ॥
sa cirāyuḥ sukhī putrī vijayī vinayī bhavet . 10 .

______________:Today's Date

स च्चिरायुः सुखी पुत्री विजयी विनयी भवेत् ॥ १० ॥

sa cirāyuḥ sukhī putrī vijayī vinayī bhavet . 10 .

Blessed souls who recite this Hymn—replete with the potency of Lord Rāma—lead long prosperous lives, fortified full of blessings: such as longevity, happiness, progeny, success, humility.

Today's Date : ____________

राम राम

पातालभूतलव्योम

चारिणश्छद्मचारिणः

।

pātāla bhūtala vyoma cāriṇa

śchadma cāriṇaḥ ,

पातालभूतलव्योमचारिणश्छद्मचारिणः ।

pātāla bhūtala vyoma cāriṇa śchadma cāriṇaḥ ,

न द्रष्टुमपि शक्तास्ते रक्षितं रामनामभिः ॥ ११ ॥

na draṣṭu mapi śakt āste rakṣitaṁ rāma nāma bhiḥ . 11 .

_______________ :Today's Date

न द्रष्टुमपि शक्तास्ते
रक्षितं रामनामभिः

॥ ११ ॥

na draṣṭumapi śaktāste
rakṣitaṁ rāmanāma
bhiḥ . 11 .

Evil spirits that travel secretly changing forms—the hidden wanderers of earth, heaven, and hell—can not even catch a glimpse of those who stand protected by the power of the chant of Rāma-Nāma.

राम राम

राम राम

रामेति रामभद्रेति रामच्चन्द्रेति वा स्मरन् ।

rāmeti rāma bhadreti rāma candreti vā smaran ,

रामेति रामभद्रेति रामचन्द्रेति वा स्मरन् ।

rāmeti rāma bhadreti rāma candreti vā smaran ,

नरो न लिप्यते पापैभुक्तिं मुक्तिं च विन्दति ॥ १२ ॥

naro na lipyate pāpai bhuktiṁ muktiṁ ca vindati . 12 .

_______________ Today's Date

राम राम

राम राम

नरो न लिप्यते
पापैभुक्तिं मुक्तिं च
विन्दति ॥ १२ ॥

naro na lipyate pāpai
bhuktiṁ muktiṁ ca
vindati . 12 .

People who continually reflect upon His names: like Rāma, Rāmbhadra, Rāmachandra, never get entangled in sin; and with ease they attain the aim of their choosing—be it final emancipation, or a zestful worldly life.

Today's Date : ______________

राम राम

राम राम

जगज्जैत्रेकमन्त्रेण

रामनाम्ना

ऽभिरक्षितम् ।

jagajjaitrekamantreṇa rāma nāmnā 'bhirakṣitam ,

जगज्जैत्रेकमन्त्रेण रामनाम्नाऽभिरक्षितम् ।

jagajjai trekam antreṇa rāma nāmnā 'bhirakṣ itam ,

यः कण्ठे धारयेत्तस्य करस्थाः सर्वसिद्धयः ॥ १३ ॥

yaḥ kaṇṭhe dhāra yettasya kara sthāḥ sarva siddha yaḥ . 13 .

________________:Today's Date

राम राम

राम राम

यः कण्ठे धारयेत्तस्य
करस्थाः सर्वसिद्धयः
॥ १३ ॥

yaḥ kaṇṭhe dhārayettasya
karasthāḥ sarva siddha
yaḥ . 13 .

They who wear on their neck [memorize] this Hymn—the sole world-winning Mantra—get all *Siddhis* (supernatural powers) within their grasp.

राम राम

वज्रपंजरनामेदं यो

रामकवचं स्मरेत् ।

vajra paṁjara nāmedaṁ yo
rāma kavacaṁ smaret ,

राम राम

वज्रपंजरनामेदं यो रामकवचं स्मरेत् ।
vajra paṁjara nāmedaṁ yo rāma kavacaṁ smaret ,
अव्याहताज्ञः सर्वत्र लभते जयमंगलम् ॥ १४ ॥
avyā hatā jñaḥ sarvatra labhate jaya maṁgalam . 14 .

_______________:Today's Date

राम राम

अव्याहताज्ञः सर्वत्र
लभते जयमंगलम्
॥ १४ ॥

avyāhatājñaḥ sarvatra
labhate jaya maṁgalam . 14 .

Those who stand fortified by this Armor of Rāma—known as the Cage of Diamond—command obedience over all; and they remain ever victorious, ever bright, ever auspicious.

Today's Date : ____________________

राम राम

आदिष्टवान्यथा स्वप्ने रामरक्षामिमां हरः ।

ādiṣṭa vānyathā svapne rāma rakṣā mimāṁ haraḥ ,

राम राम

आदिष्टवान्यथा स्वप्ने रामरक्षामिमां हरः ।
ādiṣṭa vānyathā svapne rāma rakṣā mimāṁ haraḥ ,
तथा लिखितवान्प्रातः प्रभुद्धो बुधकौशिकः ॥ १५ ॥
tathā likhita vān prātaḥ pra bhuddho budha kauśikaḥ . 15 .

________________:Today's Date

तथा

लिखितवान्प्रातः

प्रभुद्धो बुधकौशिकः

॥ १५ ॥

tathā likhitavān prātaḥ
prabhuddho budha kauśikaḥ
. 15 .

It was in a revelation that this protective Shield-of-Rāma was divulged by Lord Shiva; and upon waking it was transcribed by Buddha-Kaushik as ordained.

राम राम

आरामः

कल्पवृक्षाणां विरामः

सकलापदाम् ।

ārāmaḥ kalpa vṛkṣāṇāṁ

virāmaḥ sakal āpadām ,

राम राम

आरामः कल्पवृक्षाणां विरामः सकलापदाम् ।
ārāmaḥ kalpa vṛkṣāṇāṁ virā maḥ sakal āpadām ,
अभिरामस्त्रिलोकानां रामः श्रीमान्स नः प्रभुः ॥ १६ ॥
abhirāmas trilok ānāṁ rāmaḥ śrī mānsa naḥ prabhuḥ . 16 .

__________ :Today's Date

राम राम

राम राम

अभिरामस्त्रिलोकानां

रामः श्रीमान्स नः

प्रभुः ॥ १६ ॥

abhirāmas trilokānāṁ rāmaḥ
śrīmānsa naḥ prabhuḥ . 16 .

He—who is the destroyer of every obstacle—who is, as it were, a grove of wish-yielding trees—who is the praise of all the three worlds—He Shrī Rāma—is our Bhagwān, Lord-God Supreme.

राम राम

राम राम

तरुणौ रूपसम्पन्नौ

सुकुमारौ महाबलौ ।

taruṇau rūpa sampannau
sukumārau mahā balau ,

तरुणौ रूपसम्पन्नौ सुकुमारौ महाबलौ ।
taruṇau rūpa sampannau su kumārau mahā balau ,
पुण्डरीकविशालाक्षौ चीरकृष्णाजिनाम्बरौ ॥ १७ ॥
puṇḍarīka viśāl ākṣau cīra kṛṣṇā jinām barau . 17 .

_______________ :Today's Date

राम राम

पुण्डरीकविशालाक्षौ
चीरकृष्णाजिनाम्बरौ
॥ १७ ॥

puṇḍarīka viśālākṣau cīra
kṛṣṇā jinām barau . 17 .

Full of beauty, charming youths mighty and strong, with lotus-like broad exquisite eyes, who have donned the bark of tree and dark deer skins—

Today's Date : ____________________

राम राम

फलमूलाशिनौ

दान्तौ तापसौ

ब्रह्मचारिणौ ।

phala mūlāśinau dāntau
tāpasau brahma cāriṇau ,

फलमूलाशिनौ दान्तौ तापसौ ब्रह्मचारिणौ ।
phala mūl āśinau dāntau tāpasau brahma cāriṇau ,
पुत्रौ दशरथस्यैतौ भ्रातरौ रामलक्ष्मणौ ॥ १८ ॥
putrau daśa ratha syaitau bhrā tarau rāma lakṣmaṇau . 18 .

________ Today's Date

पुत्रौ दशरथस्यैतौ
भ्रातरौ रामलक्ष्मणौ
॥ १८ ॥

putrau daśarathasyaitau
bhrātarau rāma
lakṣmaṇau . 18 .

—who subsist on fruits and roots who live as celibates practicing penance, those sons of Dashrath—the two brothers Rāma and Lakshman

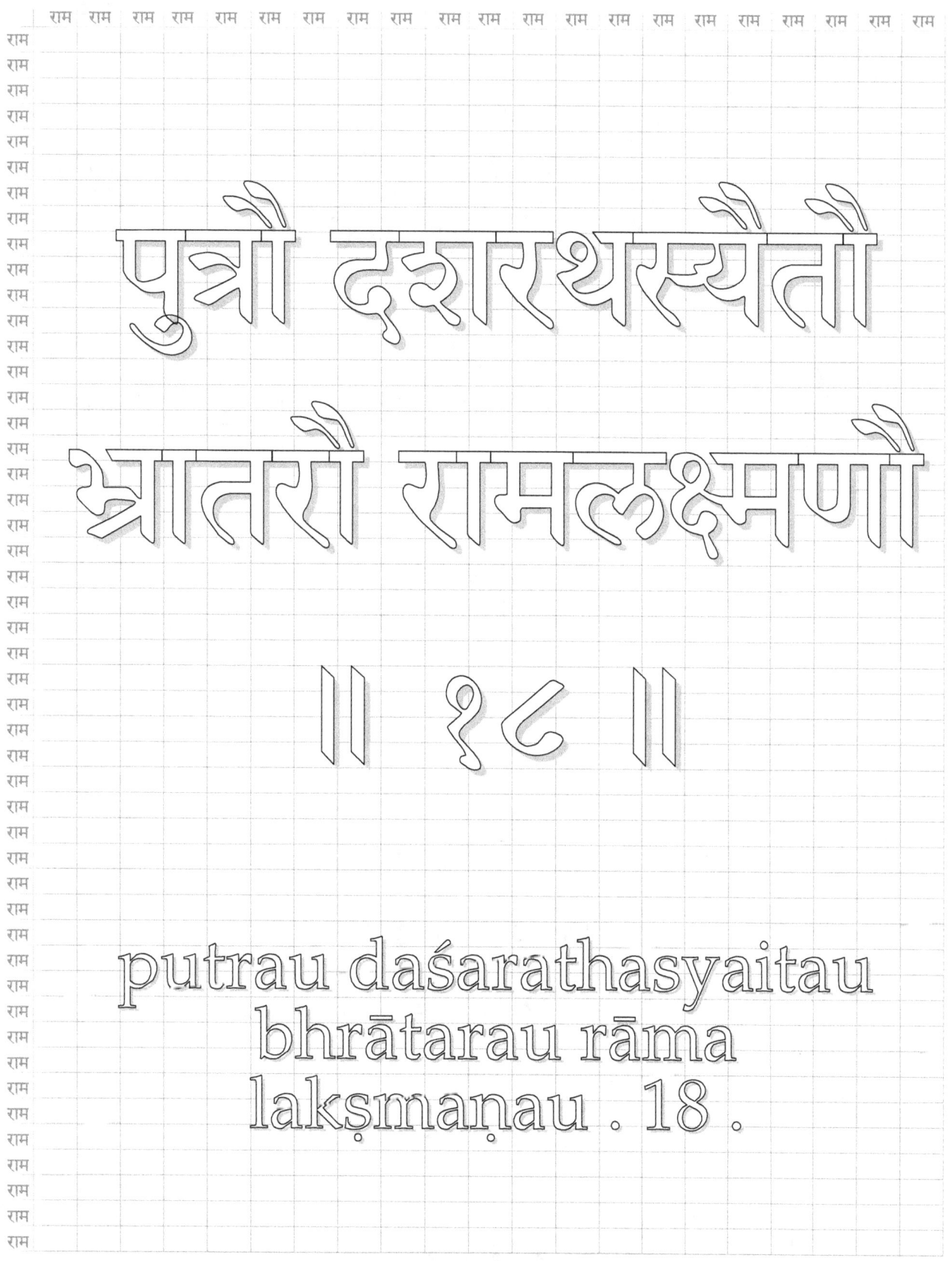

राम राम

शरण्यौ सर्वसत्त्वानां

श्रेष्ठौ सर्वधनुष्मताम्

।

śaraṇyau sarva sattvānāṁ
śreṣṭhau sarva
dhanuṣ matām ,

शरण्यौ सर्वसत्त्वानां श्रेष्ठौ सर्वधनुष्मताम् ।

śaraṇ yau sarva satt vānāṁ śre ṣṭhau sarva dhanuṣ matām ,

रक्षः कुलनिहन्तारौ त्रायेतां नो रघूत्तमौ ॥ १९ ॥

rakṣaḥ kulani hantārau trā yetāṁ no raghū ttamau . 19 .

_______________ :Today's Date

रक्षः कुलनिहन्तारौ
त्रायेतां नो रघूत्तमौ
॥ १९ ॥

rakṣaḥ kulani hantārau
trāyetāṁ no raghūttamau
. 19 .

—the foremost amongst all archers, the destroyers of whole race of demons, who give life and shelter to all beings—those best of scions of Raghus, may they grant protection to me.

राम राम

राम राम

आत्तसज्जधनुषा

विषुस्पृशा

वक्षयाशुगानिषङ्ग

सङ्गनौ ।

ātta sajja dhanuṣā viṣuspṛśā vakṣayāśuga niṣaṅga saṅganau ,

आत्तसज्जधनुषाविषुस्पृशावक्षयाशुगनिषङ्गसङ्गनौ ।

ātta sajja dhanuṣā viṣu spṛśā vakṣay āśuga niṣaṅga saṅganau ,

रक्षणाय मम रामलक्ष्मणावग्रतः पथि सदैव गच्छताम् ॥ २० ॥

rakṣ aṇāya mama rāma lakṣmaṇ āvagrataḥ pathi sadaiva gacch atām . 20 .

__________ Today's Date

राम राम

राम राम

रक्षणाय मम

रामलक्ष्मणावग्रतः

पथि सदैव गच्छताम्

॥ २० ॥

rakṣaṇāya mama rāma
lakṣmaṇā vagrataḥ pathi
sadaiva gacchatām . 20 .

Accompanying me, with bows pulled and ready, with their hand stroking the arrows, with quivers full of unfailing arms slung on their back—may those wayfarers Rāma and Lakshman always stay in the front—as I traverse my path—granting their protective care.

राम राम

संनद्धः कवची खड्गी

चापबाणधरो युवा ।

saṁnaddhaḥ kavacī khaḍgī
cāpa bāṇa dharo yuvā ,

संनद्धः कवची खड्गी चापबाणधरो युवा ।
saṁ naddhaḥ kavacī khaḍgī cāpa bāṇa dharo yuvā ,
गच्छन्मनोरथान्नश्च रामः पातु सलक्ष्मणः ॥ २१ ॥
gacchan manorath ānnaśca rāmaḥ pātu sa lakṣmaṇaḥ . 21 .

_______________ :Today's Date

राम राम

राम राम

गच्छन्मनोरथान्नश्च

रामः पातु

सलक्ष्मणः ॥ २१ ॥

gacchan manorathānnaśca rāmaḥ pātu sa lakṣmaṇaḥ . 21 .

Always prepared and armored—armed with bows, arrows, swords—of youthful forms—may Rāma and Lakshman always abide ahead of me, protecting my cherished thoughts.

Today's Date : ____________

राम राम

राम राम

रामो दाशरथिः शूरो लक्ष्मणानुचरो बली ।

rāmo dāśarathiḥ śūro lakṣmaṇānucaro balī ,

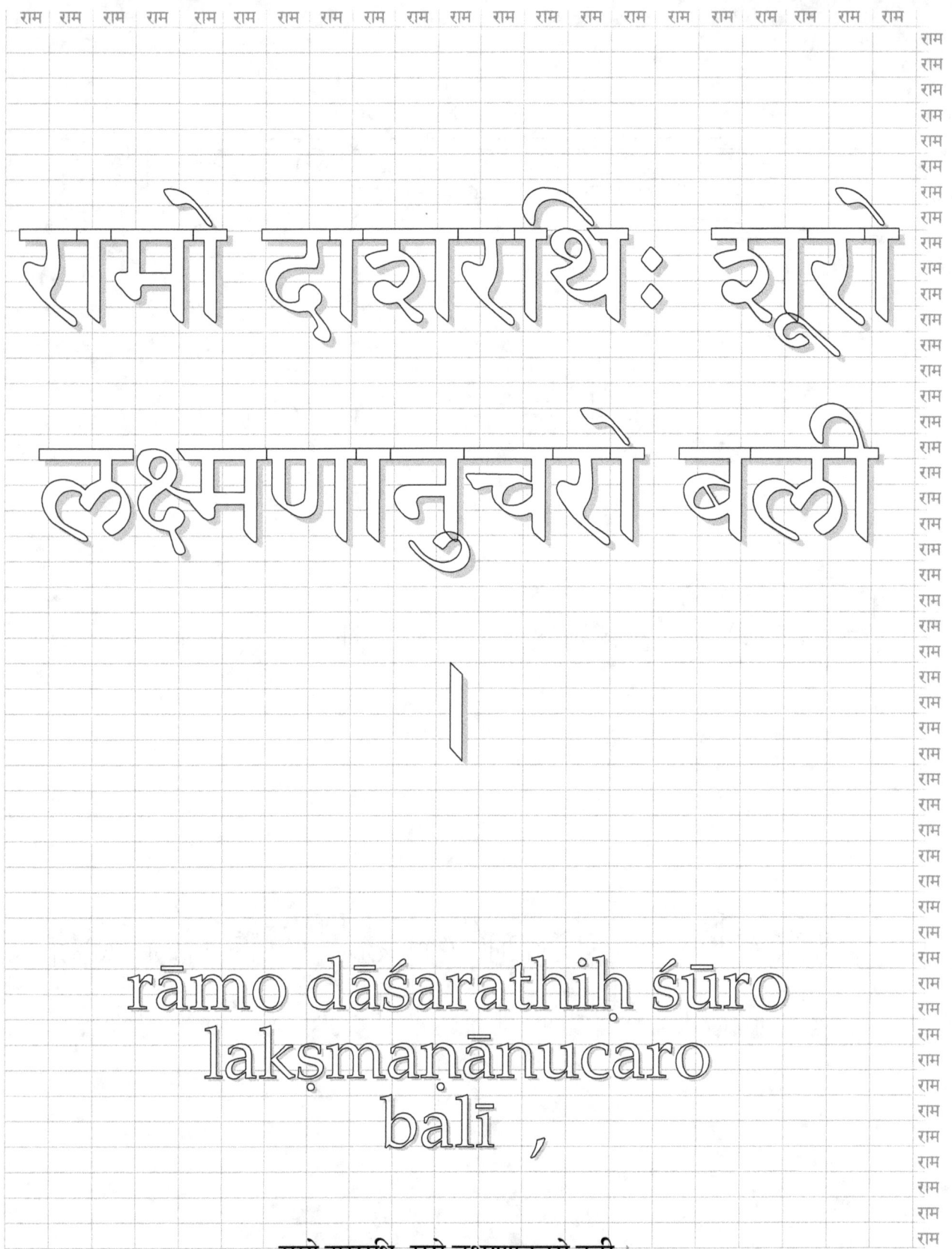

रामो दाशरथिः शूरो लक्ष्मणानुचरो बली ।
rāmo dāśarathiḥ śūro lakṣmaṇ ānucaro balī ,
काकुत्स्थः पुरुषः पूर्णः कौसल्येयो रघूत्तमः ॥ २२ ॥
kākuts thaḥ puruṣaḥ pūrṇaḥ kausal yeyo raghū ttamaḥ . 22 .

_______________ :Today's Date

राम राम

राम राम

काकुत्स्थः पुरुषः
पूर्णः कौसल्येयो
रघूत्तमः ॥ २२ ॥

kākutsthaḥ puruṣaḥ pūrṇaḥ
kausalyeyo raghūttamaḥ
. 22 .

They who recites these names of Rāma: Rāma, Dāsharathī [Dasharath's son], Shūro [Brave], Lakshman-anucharo [whom Lakshman follows], Balī [Powerful], Kākutstha [Kakutstha's Descendent], Purusha [the Supreme-Reality beyond Māyā], Pūrna [Complete], Kausalyeyo [Kausalyā's son], Raghūttama [Best of Raghus];

राम राम

राम राम

वेदान्तवेद्यो यज्ञेशः

पुराणपुरुषोत्तमः ।

vedānta vedyo yajñeśaḥ
purāṇa puruṣottamaḥ ,

वेदान्तवेद्यो यज्ञेशः पुराणपुरुषोत्तमः ।

vedānta vedyo yajñ eśaḥ purāṇa puruṣ ottamaḥ ,

जानकीवल्लभः श्रीमान् अप्रमेय पराक्रमः ॥ २३ ॥

jānakī vallabh aḥ śrī mān a prameya parā kramaḥ . 23 .

_______________:Today's Date

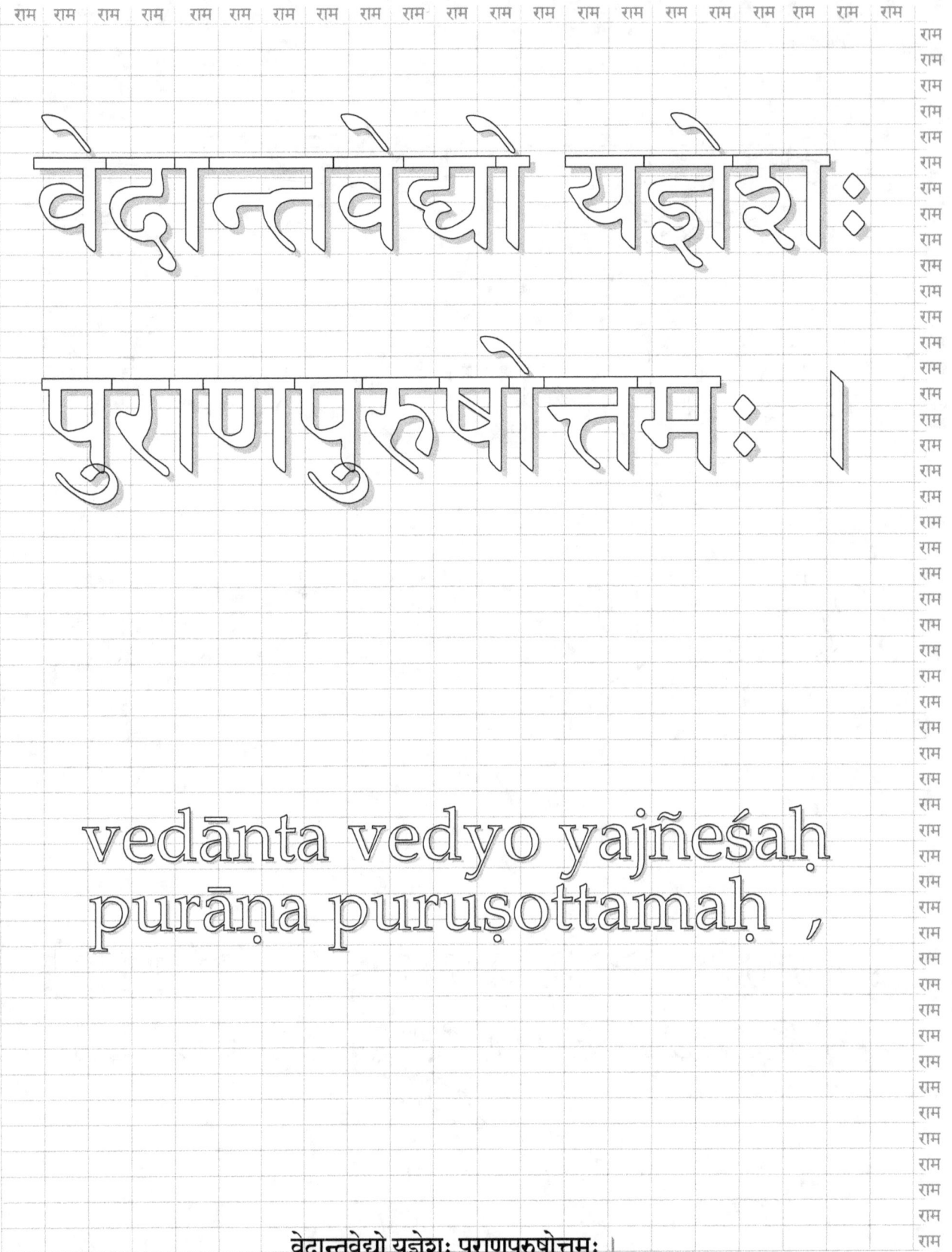

जानकीवल्लभः श्रीमान् अप्रमेय पराक्रमः ॥ २३ ॥

jānakī vallabhaḥ śrīmān
aprameya parākramaḥ . 23 .

Vedānta-Vedyo [Import of Vedanta], Yagyesha [Lord of Yagya], Purāṇa [Ancient-Most], Purushottama [Supreme-Most], Jānakī-Vallabha [Sītā's Beloved], Shrīmān [Lord of Prosperity], Aprameya-Parākrami [Immeasurably-Brave]—

राम राम

इत्येतानि जपन्नित्यं

मद्भक्तः

श्रद्धयान्वितः ।

ityetāni japannityaṁ madbhaktaḥ śraddhayānvitaḥ ,

राम राम

इत्येतानि जपन्नित्यं मद्भक्तः श्रद्धयान्वितः ।
itye tāni japan nityaṁ mad bhaktaḥ śraddha yānvitaḥ ,
अश्वमेधाधिकं पुण्यं सम्प्राप्नोति न संशयः ॥ २४ ॥
aśva medhā dhikaṁ puṇyaṁ sam prāp noti na saṁś ayaḥ . 24 .

________________ Today's Date

राम राम

राम राम

अश्वमेधाधिकं पुण्यं
सम्प्राप्नोति न संशयः
॥ २४ ॥

aśva medhādhikaṁ puṇyaṁ
samprāp noti na saṁśayaḥ
. 24 .

—they who recites these names of Rāma everyday with faith, such devotees of mine will assuredly get the fruit of Ashwamegha Yagya and more—of this let there be no doubt [says Lord Shankar].

राम राम

राम राम

रामं दुर्वादलश्यामं

पद्माक्षं पीतवाससम्

।

rāmaṁ durvādala śyāmaṁ

padmākṣaṁ pīta vāsasam ,

रामं दुर्वादलश्यामं पद्माक्षं पीतवाससम् ।

rāmaṁ durvā dala śyāmaṁ padm ākṣaṁ pīta vāsa sam ,

स्तुवन्ति नामभिर्दिव्यैर्न ते संसारिणो नराः ॥ २५ ॥

stu vanti nāmabhir div yairna te saṁ sāriṇo narāḥ . 25 .

_______________ :Today's Date

स्तुवन्ति

नामभिर्दिव्यैर्न ते

संसारिणो नराः

॥ २५ ॥

stu vanti nāmabhir divyairna te saṁ sāriṇo narāḥ . 25 .

Chanting these divine names and singing the praises of Shrī Rāma—He, who wears yellow raiments, the lotus-eyed Lord of dark complexion, of a swarthy hue as the leaves of dark *Doorba*—the faithful are never anymore trapped in the cycle of transmigration.

Today's Date : ____________________

राम राम

राम राम

रामं लक्ष्मणपूर्वजं
रघुवरं सीतापतिं
सुन्दरं

rāmaṁ lakṣmaṇa pūrvajaṁ
raghuvaraṁ sītāpatiṁ
sundaraṁ

रामं लक्ष्मणपूर्वजं रघुवरं सीतापतिं सुन्दरं

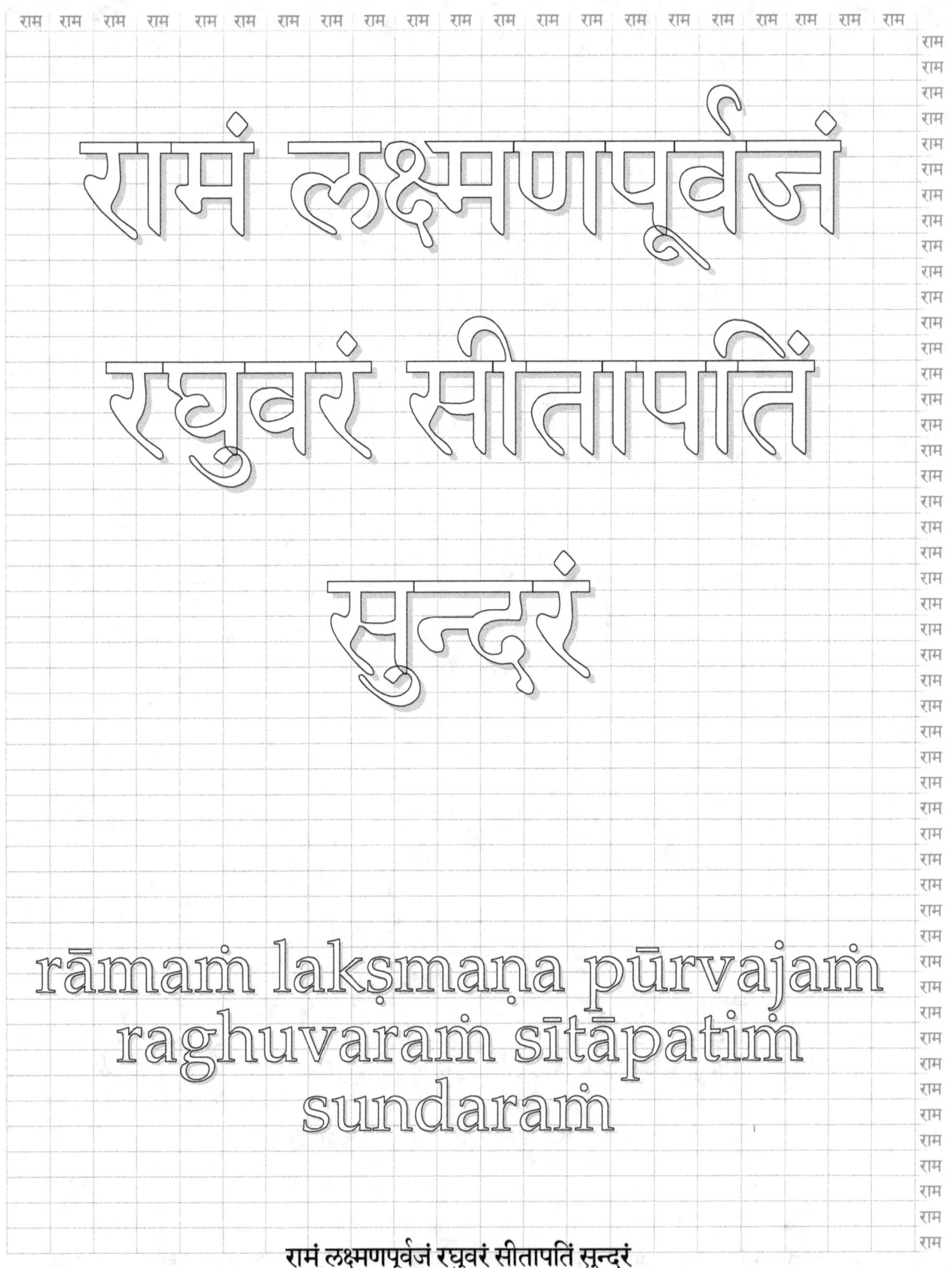

rāmaṁ lakṣmaṇa pūrvajaṁ raghu varaṁ sītā patiṁ sundaraṁ

काकुत्स्थं करुणार्णवं गुणनिधिं विप्रप्रियं धार्मिकम् ।

kākut sthaṁ karuṇār ṇavaṁ guṇa nidhiṁ vipra priyaṁ dhārmikam ,

__________________ :Today's Date

राम राम

राम राम

काकुत्स्थं करुणार्णवं
गुणनिधिं विप्रप्रियं
धार्मिकम् ।

kākutsthaṁ karuṇārṇavaṁ
guṇa nidhiṁ vipra priyaṁ
dhārmikam ,

Unto Rāma—the revered of Lakshman, the best of the House of Raghus, the most-charming Lord of Sītā, the ocean of compassion, the scion of Kakustha, a treasurehouse of virtues, the darling of the virtuous, most religious and wise;

राम राम

राम राम

राजेन्द्रं सत्यसंधं
दशरथतनयं
श्यामलं शान्तमूर्तिं

rājendraṁ satya saṁdhaṁ
daśaratha tanayaṁ
śyāmalaṁ śānta mūrtiṁ

राजेन्द्रं सत्यसंधं दशरथतनयं श्यामलं शान्तमूर्तिं

rājendraṁ satya saṁdhaṁ daśaratha tanayaṁ śyāmalaṁ śānta mūrtiṁ

वन्दे लोकाभिरामं रघुकुलतिलकं राघवं रावणारिम् ॥ २६ ॥

vande lok ābhirāmaṁ raghu kula tilakaṁ rāghavaṁ rāvaṇā rim . 26 .

________________ Today's Date

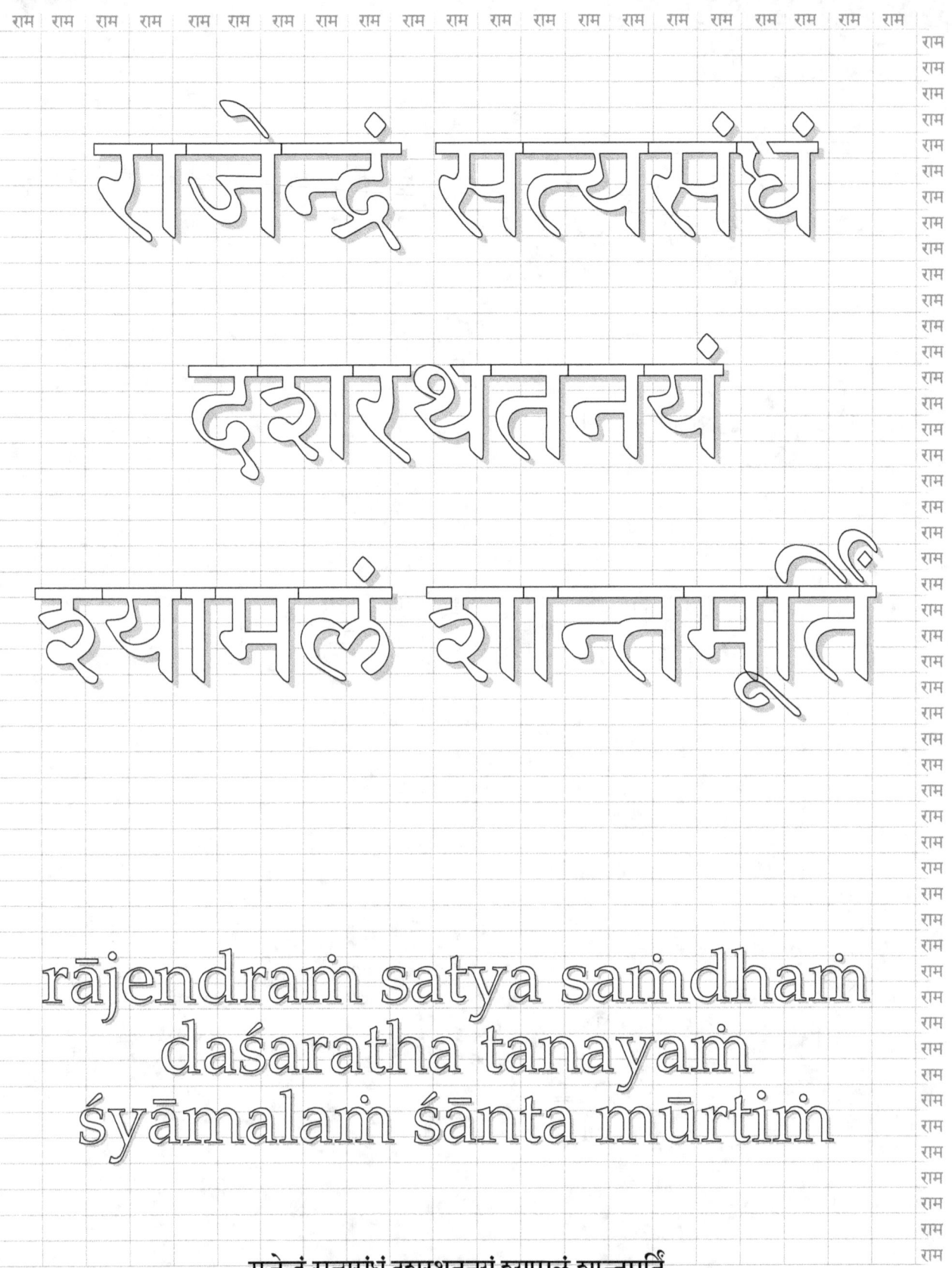

वन्दे लोकाभिरामं

रघुकुलतिलकं राघवं

रावणारिम्

॥ २६ ॥

vande lokābhirāmaṁ
raghukula tilakaṁ rāghavaṁ
rāvaṇā rim
. 26 .

who is—the Sovereign King of Kings, conjoined to Truth, the dark-complexioned son of Dashrath, Embodied-Bliss, the most exquisite in creation, the crown jewel of Raghus, slayer of the demon Rāvan—unto Him, Lord Rāghav, my repeated salutations.

Today's Date : ________________

राम राम

रामाय रामभद्राय

रामच्चन्द्राय वेधसे ।

rāmāya rāma bhadrāya rāma candrāya vedhase ,

राम राम

रामाय रामभद्राय रामचन्द्राय वेधसे ।

rāmāya rāma bhadrāya rāma candrāya vedhase ,

रघुनाथाय नाथाय सीतायाः पतये नमः ॥ २७ ॥

raghu nāthāya nāthāya sītāyāḥ pataye namaḥ . 27 .

________________ :Today's Date

राम राम

राम राग राम राम राम राम राम

रघुनाथाय नाथाय
सीतायाः पतये नमः
।। २७ ।।

raghunāthāya nāthāya
sītāyāḥ pataye namaḥ
. 27 .

I bow to Rāma; my obeisance to Rāmabhadra; my many venerations to Rāmachandra, the omniscient Lord-God Raghunāth; again and again my repeated salutations to Sītāpatī—the Lord of Sītā.

राम राम

राम
राम
राम
राम
राम
राम
राम
राम
राम
राम
राम
राम
राम
राम
राम
राम
राम
राम
राम
राम
राम
राम
राम
राम
राम
राम
राम
राम
राम
राम
राम
राम
राम
राम
राम
राम
राम
राम
राम
राम
राम
राम
राम
राम
राम
राम
राम
राम
राम
राम
राम

श्रीराम राम

रघुनन्दन राम राम

śrīrāma rāma raghunandana rāma rāma

श्रीराम राम रघुनन्दन राम राम

śrīrāma rāma raghu nandana rāma rāma

श्रीराम राम भरताग्रज राम राम ।

śrīrāma rāma bharat āgraja rāma rāma ,

________________ :Today's Date

राम राम

राम राम

श्रीराम राम
भरताग्रज राम राम
।

śrīrāma rāma bharatāgraja rāma rāma ,

I stand in surrender to Shrī Rāma—Rāma, Rāma, Raghunandan [Raghu Scion] Rāma. I give myself unto Shrī Rāma—Rāma, Rāma, Bharatāgraja [Bharat's Elder] Rāma.

Today's Date : ____________

राम राम

राम
राम
राम
राम
राम
राम
राम
राम
राम
राम
राम
राम
राम
राम
राम
राम
राम
राम
राम
राम
राम
राम
राम
राम
राम
राम
राम
राम
राम
राम
राम
राम
राम
राम
राम
राम
राम
राम
राम
राम
राम
राम
राम
राम
राम
राम
राम
राम
राम
राम

श्रीराम राम

रणकर्कश राम राम

śrīrāma rāma raṇakarkaśa
rāma rāma

श्रीराम राम रणकर्कश राम राम

śrīrāma rāma raṇa karkaśa rāma rāma

श्रीराम राम शरणं भव राम राम ॥ २८ ॥

śrīrāma rāma śaraṇaṁ bhava rāma rāma . 28 .

________________ :Today's Date

राम राम

श्रीराम राम शरणं

भव राम राम

॥ २८ ॥

śrīrāma rāma śaraṇaṁ bhava rāma rāma ॥ 28 ॥

I lay my life before Shrī Rāma—Rāma, Rāma, Rankarkasha [Terrible in Battle] Rāma. I take shelter in you O Rāma—Shrī Rāma, Rāma, Rāma; be my refuge, Lord-God.

Today's Date : ____________

राम राम

श्रीरामचन्द्रचरणौ मनसा स्मरामि

śrī rāmacandra caraṇau manasā smarāmi

राम राम

श्रीरामचन्द्रचरणौ मनसा स्मरामि

śrī rāma candra caraṇau manasā smarāmi

श्रीरामचन्द्रचरणौ वचसा गृणामि ।

śrī rāma candra caraṇau vacasā gṛṇāmi ,

_______________ :Today's Date

राम राम

राम राम

श्रीरामचन्द्रचरणौ

वचसा गृणामि ।

śrī rāmacandra caraṇau
vacasā gṛṇāmi ,

With my heart I reverence the feet of Shrī Rāmachandra. With my speech I make veneration to the holy feet of Shrī Rāmachandra.

Today's Date : ________________

राम राम

राम राम

श्रीरामचन्द्रचरणौ
शिरसा नमामि

śrī rāma candra caraṇau
śirasā namāmi

श्रीरामचन्द्रचरणौ शिरसा नमामि

śrī rāma candra caraṇau śirasā namāmi

श्रीरामचन्द्रचरणौ शरणं प्रपद्ये ॥ २९ ॥

śrī rāma candra caraṇau śaraṇaṁ prapadye . 29 .

______________ Today's Date

राम राम

राम राम

श्रीरामचन्द्रचरणौ

शरणं प्रपद्ये

॥ २९ ॥

śrī rāma candra caraṇau
śaraṇaṁ
prapadye . 29 .

With my head I salute the sacred feet of Shrī Rāma. Bowing low I take complete refuge at the holy feet of Rāma—who's a cooling moon to the burning worldly flames.

Today's Date : ______________

राम राम

राम राम

माता रामो मत्पिता रामचन्द्रः

māta rāmo mat pitā rāma candraḥ

माता रामो मत्पिता रामचन्द्रः

mātā rāmo mat pitā rāma candraḥ

स्वामी रामो मत्सखा रामचन्द्रः ।

svāmī rāmo mat sakhā rāma candraḥ ,

__________________ :Today's Date

स्वामी रामो मत्सखा रामचन्द्रः ।

svāmī rāmo matsakhā rāma candraḥ ,

Rāma is my loving mother, and Rāma my protective father. Rāma is my gracious Lord, and Rāma my beloved friend.

राम राम

सर्वस्वं मे रामचन्द्रो दयालु

sarva svaṁ me rāmacandro dayālu

राम राम

सर्वस्वं मे रामचन्द्रो दयालु

sarva svaṁ me rāma candro dayālu

नान्यं जाने नैव जाने न जाने ॥ ३० ॥

rnā nyaṁ jāne naiva jāne na jāne . 30 .

________________:Today's Date

राम राम

राम राम

नान्यं जाने नैव
जाने न जाने
॥ ३० ॥

rnānyaṁ jāne naiva jāne na jāne . 30 .

My everyone and everything is only Rāmachandra, the most-compassionate Lord. Other than Rāma I know of no other—absolutely, I know of no one except Shrī Rāma.

राम राम

राम राम

दक्षिणे लक्ष्मणो यस्य वामे च जनकात्मजा ।

dakṣiṇe lakṣmaṇo yasya vāme ca janak ātmajā ,

दक्षिणे लक्ष्मणो यस्य वामे च जनकात्मजा ।
dakṣiṇe lakṣmaṇo yasya vāme ca janak ātmajā ,
पुरतो मारुतिर्यस्य तं वन्दे रघुनन्दनम् ॥ ३१ ॥
purato mārutir yasya taṁ vande raghu nandanam . 31 .

:Today's Date

पुरतो मारुतिर्यस्य तं
वन्दे रघुनन्दनम्
॥ ३१ ॥

purato mārutir yasya taṁ
vande raghunandanam . 31 .

Who has Lakshmana to his right, and the daughter of Janaka to his left; before whom Hanumān is bowing down in reverence—to that Lord Raghu-Nandan I make my obeisance.

राम राम

राम राम

लोकाभिरामं

रणरङ्गधीरं

lokā bhirāmaṁ raṇaraṅga dhīraṁ

लोकाभिरामं रणरङ्गधीरं

lokā bhirāmaṁ raṇa raṅga dhīraṁ

राजीवनेत्रं रघुवंशनाथम् ।

rājīva netraṁ raghu vaṁśa nātham ,

__________ :Today's Date

राम राम

राजीवनेत्रं

रघुवंशनाथम् ।

rājīva netraṁ raghuvaṁśa nātham ,

The cynosure of eyes of all beings, the most valiant in battle, the lotus-eyed Lord of the Raghu-Lineage;

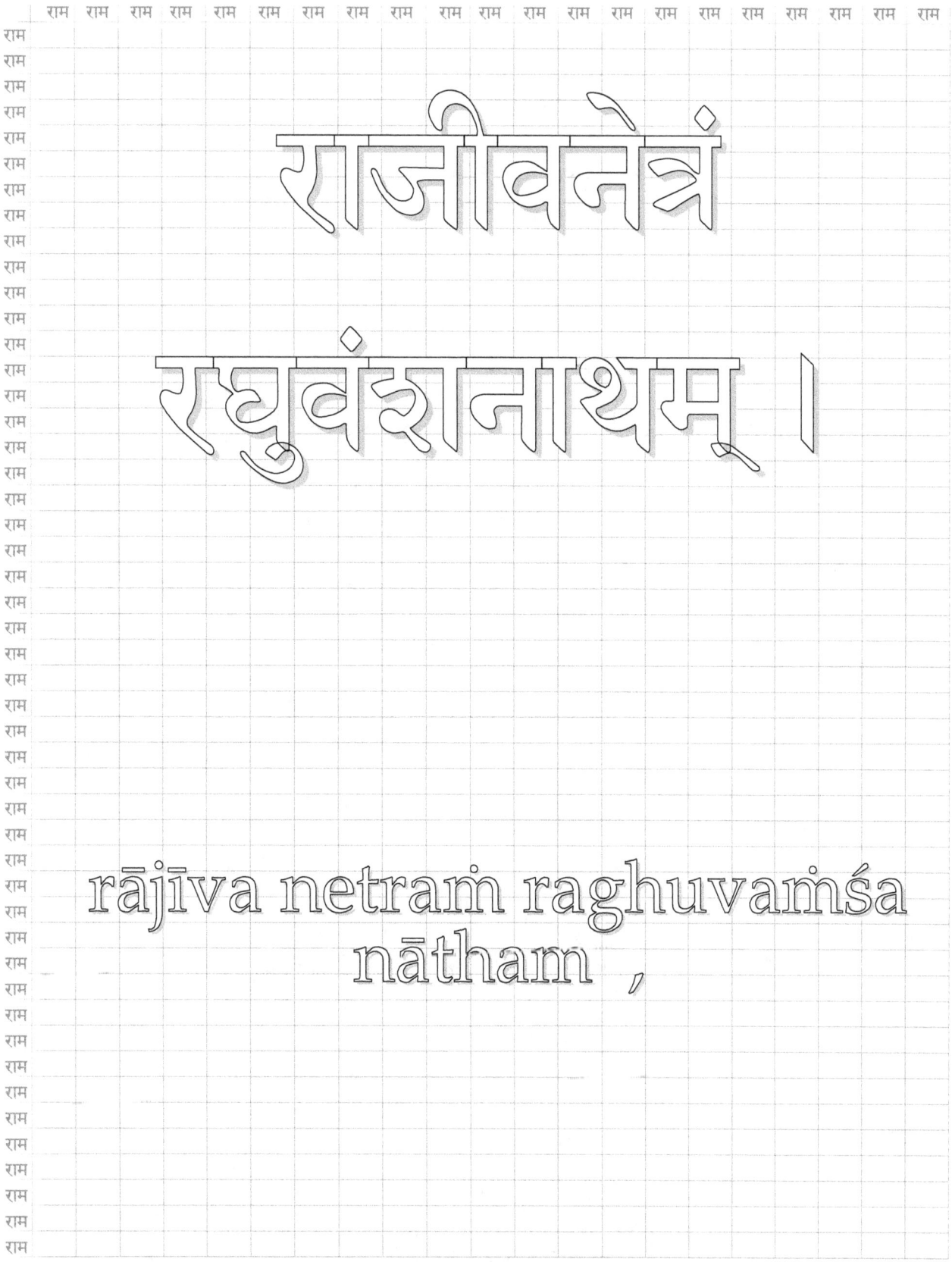

राम राम

राम राम

कारुण्यरूपं

करुणाकरं तं

kāruṇyarūpaṁ
karuṇākaraṁ taṁ

कारुण्यरूपं करुणाकरं तं

kāruṇy arūpaṁ karuṇā karaṁ taṁ

श्रीरामचन्द्रं शरणं प्रपद्ये ॥ ३२ ॥

śrī rāma candraṁ śaraṇaṁ pra padye . 32 .

________________ :Today's Date

राम राम

राम राम

श्रीरामचन्द्रं शरणं

प्रपद्ये ॥ ३२ ॥

śrī rāmacandraṁ śaraṇaṁ

pra padye . 32 .

the embodiment of compassion—unto that Lord-God Rāmachandra, in complete surrender I approach.

Today's Date : ____________________

राम राम

राम राम

मनोजवं

मारुततुल्यवेगं

manojavaṁ māruta tulya vegaṁ

मनोजवं मारुततुल्यवेगं

mano javaṁ māruta tulya vegaṁ

जितेन्द्रियं बुद्धिमतां वरिष्ठम् ।

jit endriyaṁ buddhi matāṁ vari ṣṭham ,

_______________ :Today's Date

राम राम

राम राम

जितेन्द्रियं बुद्धिमतां वरिष्ठम् ।

jitendriyaṁ buddhi matāṁ variṣṭham ,

Who is quick as the mind and equal to his sire (the Wind) in speed—unto him—who is the master of his senses and the foremost amongst the wise;

राम राम

राम राम

वातात्मजं

वानरयूथमुख्यं

vātātmajaṁ vānarayūtha mukhyaṁ

वातात्मजं वानरयूथमुख्यं

vāt ātmajaṁ vānara yūtha mukhyaṁ

श्रीरामदूतं शरणं प्रपद्ये ॥ ३३ ॥

śrī rāma dūtaṁ śaraṇaṁ pra padye . 33 .

_______________:Today's Date

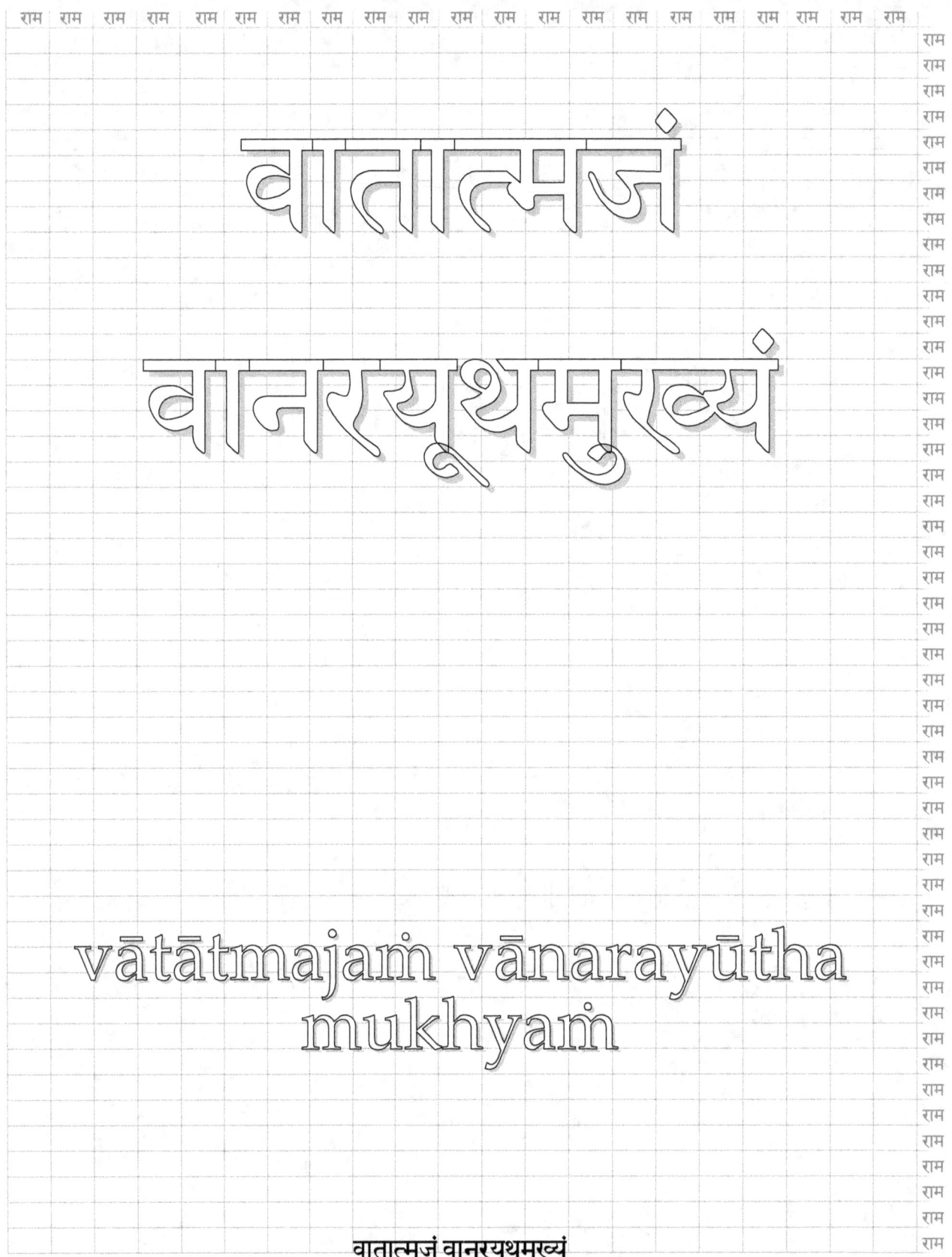

श्रीरामदूतं शरणं

प्रपद्ये ॥ ३३ ॥

śrī rāma dūtaṁ śaraṇaṁ
prapadye . 33 .

unto him—the Son-of-Wind, the chief of monkey hosts—unto that messenger of Lord Rāma—Shrī Hanumān, I come seeking refuge.

राम राम

राम राम

कूजन्तं रामरामेति

मधुरं मधुराक्षरम् ।

kūjantaṁ rāma rāmeti

madhuraṁ madhurākṣaram

,

कूजन्तं रामरामेति मधुरं मधुराक्षरम् ।

kū jantaṁ rāma rāmeti madhuraṁ madhu rākṣaram ,

आरुह्य कविताशाखां वन्दे वाल्मीकिकोकिलम् ॥ ३४ ॥

āruhya kavitā śākhāṁ vande vālmīki kokilam . 34 .

________________ :Today's Date

राम राम

आरुह्य
कविताशाखां वन्दे
वाल्मीकिकोकिलम्
॥ ३४ ॥

āruhya kavitā śākhāṁ vande
vālmīki kokilam . 34 .

He—who sports in the woods of the glories of Sītā-Rāma, like a *koel*: ever singing the sweet name of Rāma sitting on the branches of poesy—to him, the grand sage Vālmiki, I offer my salutations.

राम राम

राम राम

आपदामपहर्तारं

दातारं सर्वसम्पदाम्

।

āpadāmapahartāraṁ
dātāraṁ sarva sampadām ,

आपदामपहर्तारं दातारं सर्वसम्पदाम् ।
āpadā mapa hartāraṁ dātā raṁ sarva sampadām ,
लोकाभिरामं श्रीरामं भूयो भूयो नमाम्यहम् ॥ ३५ ॥
lokā bhirāmaṁ śrī rāmaṁ bhūyo bhūyo namām yaham . 35 .

_______________ :Today's Date

राम राम

राम राम

लोकाभिरामं श्रीरामं

भूयो भूयो

नमाम्यहम्

॥ ३५ ॥

lokābhirāmamṁ śrīrāmamṁ

bhūyo bhūyo namām yaham

. 35 .

Unto Shrī Rāma—who takes away all perils and difficulties, who is the bestower of all prosperities and prayers, who is the most beloved of all beings in the world—I bow; and I bow repeatedly.

Today's Date: ____________________

राम राम

भर्जनं

भवबीजानामर्जनं

सुखसम्पदाम् ।

bharjanaṁ bhavabījānām arjanaṁ sukha sampadām ,

राम राम

भर्जनं भवबीजानामर्जनं सुखसम्पदाम् ।

bhar janaṁ bhava bījā nāmar janaṁ sukha sam padām ,

तर्जनं यमदूतानां रामरामेति गर्जनम् ॥ ३६ ॥

tar janaṁ yama dūtā nāṁ rāma rāmeti gar janam . 36 .

______________ :Today's Date

तर्जनं यमदूतानां

राम रामेति गर्जनम्

॥ ३६ ॥

tarjanaṁ yama dūtā nāṁ

rāma rāmeti gar janam . 36 .

The chants of the name of Rāma is the fiery thunder that destructs the seed of cycle of transmigration; it is the bestower of all felicity and wealth; and it puts fear into the heart of the messenger-of-death.

राम राम

राम राम

रामो राजमणिः सदा

विजयते रामं रमेशं

भजे

rāmo rājamaṇiḥ sadā

vijayate rāmaṁ rameśaṁ

bhaje

रामो राजमणिः सदा विजयते रामं रमेशं भजे

rāmo rāja maṇiḥ sadā vijayate rāmaṁ rameśaṁ bhaje

रामेणाभिहता निशाचरचमू रामाय तस्मै नमः ।

rāmeṇ ābhihatā niśā cara camū rāmāya tasmai namaḥ ,

_______________:Today's Date

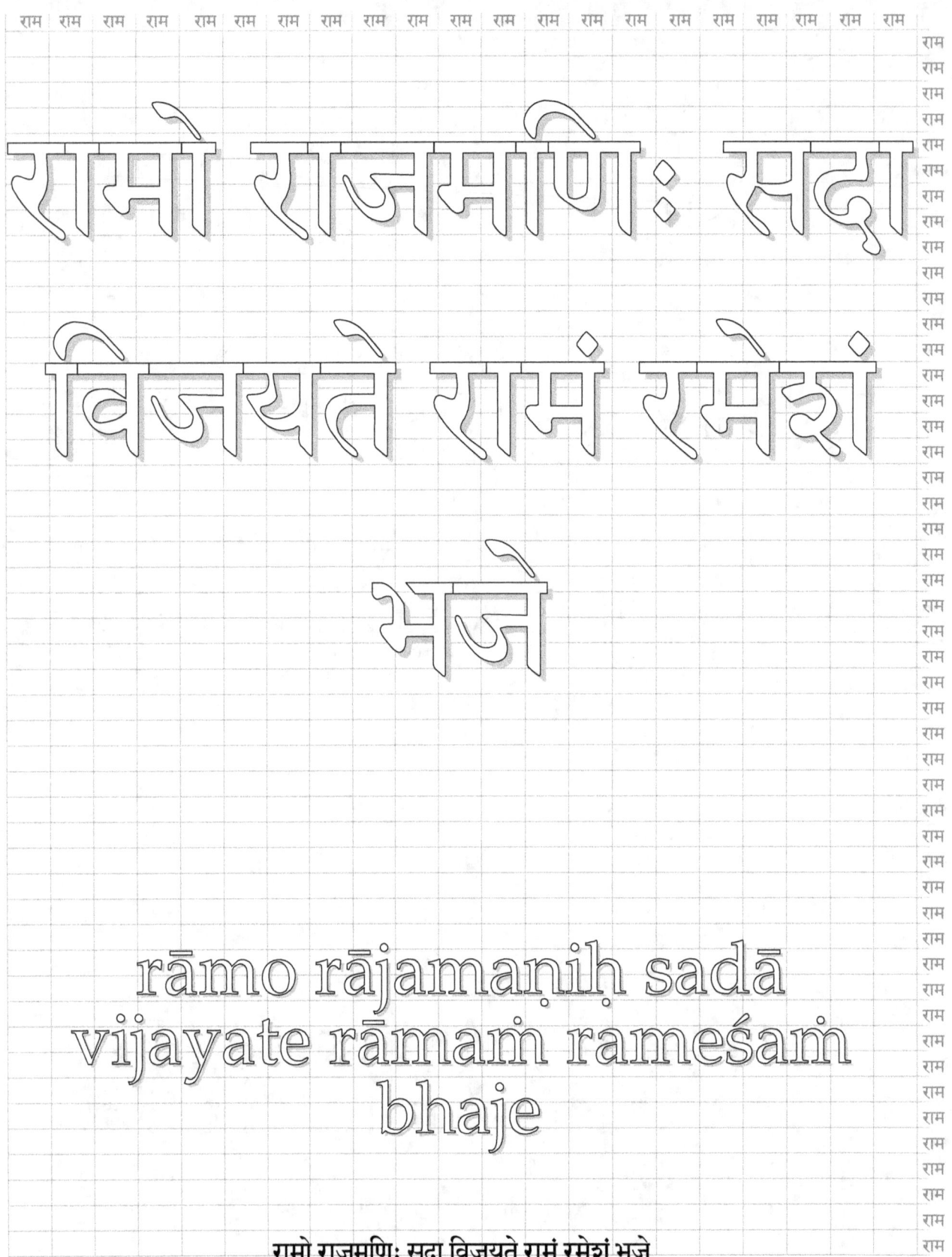

राम राम

रामेणाभिहता
निशाचरच्चमू रामाय
तस्मै नमः ।

rāmeṇ ābhihatā niśācara
camū rāmāya tasmai namaḥ

Rāma, the Crest-Jewel of Monarchs, is ever victorious. I sing the praises of Shrī Rāma, Lord of all beings. He Rāma, who decimated the whole army of night-roving demons, Him I devoutly revere.

राम राम

रामान्नास्ति परायणं
परतरं रामस्य
दासोऽस्म्यहं

rāmānnāsti parāyaṇaṁ paratараṁ rāmasya dāso 'smyahaṁ

राम राम

रामान्नास्ति परायणं परतरं रामस्य दासोऽस्म्यहं

rāmān nāsti parā yaṇaṁ parataraṁ rāmasya dāso 'smyahaṁ

रामे चित्तलयः सदा भवतु मे भो राम मामुद्धर ॥ ३७ ॥

rāme citta layaḥ sadā bhavatu me bho rāma mām uddhara . 37 .

_______________:Today's Date

राम राम

रामे चित्तलयः सदा

भवतु मे भो राम

मामुद्धर ॥ ३७ ॥

rāme cittalayaḥ sadā bhavatu
me bho rāma māmuddhara
. 37 .

There is no greater refuge than Rāma; I am a servant of Shrī Rāma. My mind remains ever absorbed in Rāma. O Rāma Lord-God, please redeem me.

राम राम

राम राम

राम रामेति रामेति
रमे रामे मनोरमे ।

rāma rāmeti rāmeti rame
rāme manorame ,

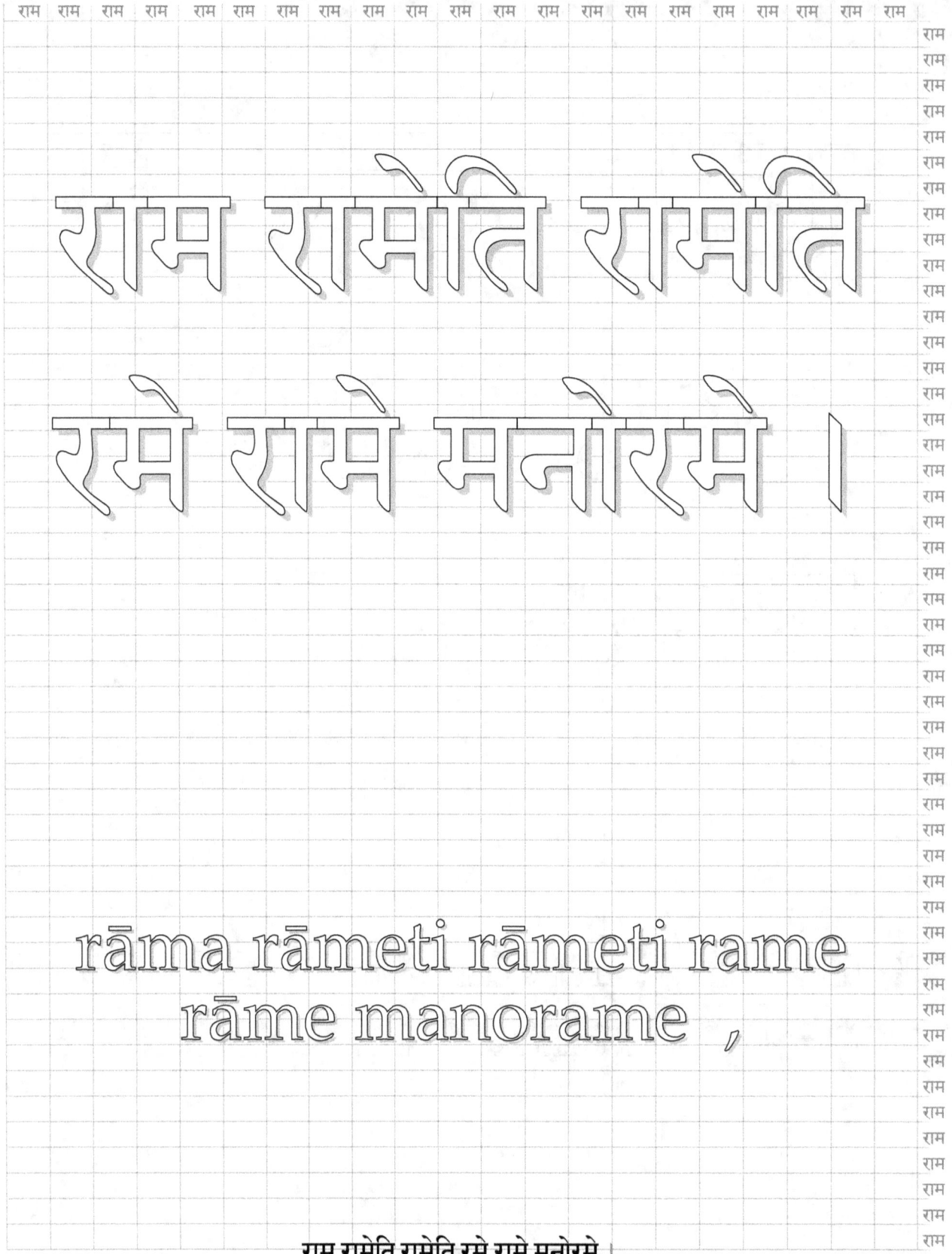

राम रामेति रामेति रमे रामे मनोरमे ।
rāma rāmeti rāmeti rame rāme mano rame ,
सहस्रनाम तत्तुल्यं रामनाम वरानने ॥ ३८ ॥
sahasra nāma tat tulyaṁ rāma nāma varā nane . 38 .

________________: Today's Date

राम राम

राम राम

सहस्रनाम तत्तुल्यं
रामनाम वरानने
॥ ३८ ॥

sahasra nāma tat tulyaṁ
rāma nāma varā nane . 38 .

Rāma, Rāma, Rāma—chanting this beautiful Name Rāma, my mind remains ever absorbed in God. The one name 'Rāma' is equivalent to a thousand other names of God, O fair-faced [Umā—says Shiva].

Today's Date : ____________

राम राम

राम
राम
राम
राम
राम
राम
राम
राम
राम
राम
राम
राम
राम
राम
राम
राम
राम
राम
राम
राम
राम
राम
राम
राम
राम
राम
राम
राम
राम
राम
राम
राम
राम
राम
राम
राम
राम
राम
राम
राम
राम
राम
राम
राम
राम
राम
राम
राम

राम

॥ इति श्रीबुधकौशिकमुनिविरचितं श्रीरामरक्षास्तोत्रं सम्पूर्णम् ॥

. iti śrī-budha-kauśika-muni-viraci-taṁ śrī-rāma-rakṣā-stotraṁ sam-pūrṇam .

__________________: Today's Date

राम राम

राम
राम
राम
राम
राम
राम
राम
राम
राम
राम
राम
राम
राम
राम
राम
राम
राम
राम
राम
राम
राम
राम
राम
राम
राम
राम
राम
राम
राम
राम
राम
राम
राम
राम
राम
राम
राम
राम
राम
राम
राम
राम
राम
राम
राम
राम
राम
राम

राम

— Thus concludes Rāma-rakshāstotra composed by Shrī Buddha-Kaushik Muni —

Today's Date : ________________

राम राम

राम

राम
राम
राम
राम
राम
राम
राम
राम
राम
राम
राम
राम
राम
राम
राम
राम
राम
राम
राम
राम
राम
राम
राम
राम
राम
राम
राम
राम
राम
राम
राम
राम
राम
राम
राम
राम
राम
राम
राम
राम
राम
राम
राम
राम
राम
राम
राम
राम

________________ :Today's Date

राम राम

राम
राम
राम
राम
राम
राम
राम
राम
राम
राम
राम
राम
राम
राम
राम
राम
राम
राम
राम
राम
राम
राम
राम
राम
राम
राम
राम
राम
राम
राम
राम
राम
राम
राम
राम
राम
राम
राम
राम
राम
राम
राम
राम
राम
राम
राम
राम
राम

राम

राम राम

राम
राम
राम
राम
राम
राम
राम
राम
राम
राम
राम
राम
राम
राम
राम
राम
राम
राम
राम
राम
राम
राम
राम
राम
राम
राम
राम
राम
राम
राम
राम
राम
राम
राम
राम
राम
राम
राम
राम
राम
राम
राम
राम
राम
राम
राम
राम
राम

राम

________________ :Today's Date

राम राम

राम
राम
राम
राम
राम
राम
राम
राम
राम
राम
राम
राम
राम
राम
राम
राम
राम
राम
राम
राम
राम
राम
राम
राम
राम
राम
राम
राम
राम
राम
राम
राम
राम
राम
राम
राग
राम
राम
राम
राम
राम
राम
राम
राम
राम
राम
राम
राम

राम

राम राम

राम
राम
राम
राम
राम
राम
राम
राम
राम
राम
राम
राम
राम
राम
राम
राम
राम
राम
राम
राम
राम
राम
राम
राम
राम
राम
राम
राम
राम
राम
राम
राम
राम
राम
राम
राम
राम
राम
राम
राम
राम
राम
राम
राम
राम
राम
राम
राम

__________________:Today's Date

श्रीरामरक्षास्तोत्र

śrī-rāma-rakṣā-stotra

अस्य श्रीरामरक्षास्तोत्रमन्त्रस्य बुधकौशिक ऋषिः
asya śrī rāma rakṣāstotra mantrasya budha kauśika ṛṣiḥ
श्रीसीतारामचन्द्रो देवता अनुष्टुप् छन्दः
śrī sītā rāma candro devatā anuṣṭup chandaḥ
सीता शक्तिः श्रीमान् हनुमान् कीलकं
sītā śaktiḥ śrīmān hanumān kīlakaṁ
श्रीरामचन्द्रप्रीत्यर्थे रामरक्षास्तोत्रजपे विनियोगः ॥
śrī rāma candra prītyarthe rāma rakṣā stotra jape viniyogaḥ .

Trans:

Of this Rāmrakshāstotra (**Hymn-of-Rāma**—for gaining **Protection**) the *Rishi* is: Buddha-Kaushik; the eight syllable quarter *Anushthap* is: the Meter; and the Deity: **Shrī Sītā-Ramachandra**. **Shrī Sītā** is the underlying energy: *Shakti*; and **Shrī Hanumān**: the anchor; the usage is: Recitation. This Rāmrakshāstotra is invoked through recitation—to please Shrī Ramachandra and earn His benediction and grace.

-- अथ ध्यानम् . *atha dhyānam* --
-- [**Meditate**] --

ध्यायेदाजानुबाहुं धृतशरधनुषं बद्धपद्मासनस्थं
dhyāye dājānu bāhuṁ dhṛta śara dhanuṣaṁ baddha padmā sanasthaṁ
पीतं वासो वसानं नवकमलदलस्पर्धिनेत्रं प्रसन्नम् ।
pītaṁ vāso vasānaṁ nava kamala dala spardhi netraṁ prasannam ,
वामाङ्करूढसीतामुखकमलमिलल्लोचनं नीरदाभं
vāmāṅka rūḍha sītā mukha kamala mila llocanaṁ nīra dābhaṁ
नानालंकारदीप्तं दधतमुरुजटामण्डलं रामचन्द्रम् ॥
nānā laṁkāra dīptaṁ dadhata murujaṭā maṇḍalaṁ rāma candram .

Trans:

Meditate upon Him: of abundant arms, holding bow and arrows in His hands, donning yellow apparels, seated in a lotus posture; of a beaming countenance, whose exquisite eyes—which compete with the petals of fresh lotus—are locked on the lovely lotus-faced Sītā sitting to his left. Upon Him—of a hue dark as heavy rain-clouds, crowned with long dense matted hair, who shines resplendent with several ornaments—upon Him, Bhagwan Shrī Ramachandra, meditate.

-- इति ध्यानम् . *iti dhyānam* --
-- [Meditation concludes (Mantras Begin)] --

चरितं रघुनाथस्य शतकोटि प्रविस्तरम् ।
caritaṁ raghu nāthasya śata koṭi pravis taram ,
एकैकमक्षरं पुंसां महापातकनाशनम् ॥ १ ॥
ek aikam akṣaraṁ puṁsāṁ mahā pātaka nāśa nam . 1 .

Trans:

Illimitable the resplendent glory of Raghunāth, a hundred billion words in extent—each and every word of which destructs the most grievous sin.

ध्यात्वा नीलोत्पलश्यामं रामं राजीवलोचनम् ।
dhyā tvā nīl otpala śyāmaṁ rāmaṁ rājīva locanam ,

जानकीलक्ष्मणोपेतं जटामुकुटमण्डितम् ॥ २ ॥
jānakī lakṣmaṇo petaṁ jaṭā mukuṭa maṇḍitam . 2 .

सासितूणधनुर्बाणपाणिं नक्तंचरान्तकम् ।
sāsitūṇa dhanur bāṇa pāṇiṁ naktaṁ carāntakam ,

स्वलीलया जगत्त्रातुमविर्भूतमजं विभुम् ॥ ३ ॥
sva līlayā jagat trātuma virbhūta majaṁ vibhum . 3 .

रामरक्षां पठेत्प्राज्ञः पापघ्नीं सर्वकामदाम् ।
rāma rakṣāṁ paṭhet prājñaḥ pāpa ghnīṁ sarva kāma dām ,

शिरो मे राघवः पातु भालं दशरथात्मजः ॥ ४ ॥
śiro me rāghavaḥ pātu bhālaṁ daśarath ātmajaḥ . 4 .

Trans:

Meditating upon Him—of a hue that is a dark blue, with eyes like a pair of lotuses, well-adorned with a crown of matted hair; who wields sword, bow and arrows, the destroyer of demons; who, though birthless, of his own will became Incarnate to protect the world—meditating upon Him: Shrī Rāma accompanied by Sītā and Lakshman—the wise recite this Rāmrakshāstotra—which destroys all sins, grants every desire, and bestows God's protection. Now then I pray: May Rāghav guard the head; may Dasharatha's son protect the forehead.

कौसल्येयो दृशौ पातु विश्वामित्रप्रियः श्रुती ।
kausal yeyo dṛśau pātu viśvā mitra priyaḥ śrutī ,

घ्राणं पातु मखत्राता मुखं सौमित्रिवत्सलः ॥ ५ ॥
ghrāṇaṁ pātu makha trātā mukhaṁ saumitri vatsalaḥ . 5 .

Trans:

May the eyes stand protected by the son of Kausalyā; the ears by the favorite disciple of Vishwāmitra; the nasals by the savior of sacrificial fires; the mouth by Him who is most affectionate to the son of Sumitrā.

जिह्वां विद्यानिधिः पातु कण्ठं भरतवंदितः ।
jihvāṁ vidyā nidhiḥ pātu kaṇṭhaṁ bharata vaṁditaḥ ,

स्कन्धौ दिव्यायुधः पातु भुजौ भग्नेशकार्मुकः ॥ ६ ॥
skandhau divyā yudhaḥ pātu bhujau bhag neśa kārmukaḥ . 6 .

Trans:

May the ocean-of-wisdom protect the tongue; Bharat's Lord the neck. May the wielder of celestial weapons shield the shoulders; may the arms be fortified by His mighty arms who effortlessly broke the Bow of Shankara.

करौ सीतापतिः पातु हृदयं जामदग्न्यजित् ।
karau sītā patiḥ pātu hṛdayaṁ jāma dagnya jit ,

मध्यं पातु खरध्वंसी नाभिं जाम्बवदाश्रयः ॥ ७ ॥
madhyaṁ pātu khara dhvaṁsī nābhiṁ jāmbavad āśrayaḥ . 7 .

Trans:

May the Lord of Sītā protect the hands; may He, who won over Parshurām, protect the heart; may the middle be preserved by the slayer of demon Khara; may He, who gave shelter to Jāmvant, shelter the navel.

सुग्रीवेशः कटी पातु सक्थिनी हनुमत्प्रभुः ।
sugrī veśaḥ kaṭī pātu sakthinī hanumat prabhuḥ ,

ऊरू रघूत्तमः पातु रक्षःकुलविनाशकृत् ॥ ८ ॥
ūrū raghū ttamaḥ pātu rakṣaḥ kula vināśakṛt . 8 .
Trans:
May the Master of Sugrīva protects the waist; may the Lord of Hanumān protect the hips. May the laps stand protected by the best of Raghus scion—who is the destroyer of lineage of demons.

जानुनी सेतुकृत्पातु जङ्घे दशमुखान्तकः ।
jānunī setu kṛtpātu jaṅaghe daśa mukh āntakaḥ ,
पादौ बिभीषणश्रीदः पातु रामोऽखिलं वपुः ॥ ९ ॥
pādau bibhīṣaṇ aśrīdaḥ pātu rām o'khilaṁ vapuḥ . 9 .
Trans:
May He, who spanned a bridge across the sea—guard the knees; may the slayer of the Ten-Headed demon—protect the shins; may the bestower of kingdom to Vibhīshan—protect the feet. May Shrī Rāma be the armor of the entire body.

एतां रामबलोपेतां रक्षां यः सुकृती पठेत् ।
etāṁ rāma balo petāṁ rakṣāṁ yaḥ sukṛtī paṭhet ,
स चिरायुः सुखी पुत्री विजयी विनयी भवेत् ॥ १० ॥
sa cirāyuḥ sukhī putrī vijayī vinayī bhavet . 10 .
Trans:
Blessed souls who recite this Hymn—replete with the potency of Lord Rāma—lead long prosperous lives, fortified full of blessings: such as longevity, happiness, progeny, success, humility.

पातालभूतलव्योमचारिणश्छद्मचारिणः ।
pātāla bhūtala vyoma cāriṇa śchadma cāriṇaḥ ,
न द्रष्टुमपि शक्तास्ते रक्षितं रामनामभिः ॥ ११ ॥
na draṣṭu mapi śakt āste rakṣitaṁ rāma nāma bhiḥ . 11 .
Trans:
Evil spirits that travel secretly changing forms—the hidden wanderers of earth, heaven, and hell—can not even catch a glimpse of those who stand protected by the power of the chant of Rāma-Nāma.

रामेति रामभद्रेति रामचन्द्रेति वा स्मरन् ।
rāmeti rāma bhadreti rāma candreti vā smaran ,
नरो न लिप्यते पापैभुक्तिं मुक्तिं च विन्दति ॥ १२ ॥
naro na lipyate pāpai bhuktiṁ muktiṁ ca vindati . 12 .
Trans:
People who continually reflect upon His names: like Rāma, Rāmbhadra, Rāmachandra, never get entangled in sin; and with ease they attain the aim of their choosing—be it final emancipation, or a zestful worldly life.

जगज्जैत्रेकमन्त्रेण रामनाम्नाऽभिरक्षितम् ।
jagajjai trekam antreṇa rāma nāmnā 'bhirakṣ itam ,
यः कण्ठे धारयेत्तस्य करस्थाः सर्वसिद्धयः ॥ १३ ॥
yaḥ kaṇṭhe dhāra yettasya kara sthāḥ sarva siddha yaḥ . 13 .
Trans:
They who wear on their neck [memorize] this Hymn—the sole world-winning Mantra—get all *Siddhis* (supernatural powers) within their grasp.

वज्रपंजरनामेदं यो रामकवचं स्मरेत् ।
vajra paṁjara nāmedaṁ yo rāma kavacaṁ smaret ,

अव्याहताज्ञः सर्वत्र लभते जयमंगलम् ॥ १४ ॥

avyā hatā jñaḥ sarvatra labhate jaya maṁgalam . 14 .

Trans:

Those who stand fortified by this Armor of Rāma—known as the Cage of Diamond—command obedience over all; and they remain ever victorious, ever bright, ever auspicious.

आदिष्टवान्यथा स्वप्ने रामरक्षामिमां हरः ।

ādiṣṭa vānyathā svapne rāma rakṣā mimāṁ haraḥ ,

तथा लिखितवान्प्रातः प्रभुद्धो बुधकौशिकः ॥ १५ ॥

tathā likhita vān prātaḥ pra bhuddho budha kauśikaḥ . 15 .

Trans:

It was in a revelation that this protective Shield-of-Rāma was divulged by Lord Shiva; and upon waking it was transcribed by Buddha-Kaushik as ordained.

आरामः कल्पवृक्षाणां विरामः सकलापदाम् ।

ārāmaḥ kalpa vṛkṣāṇāṁ virā maḥ sakal āpadām ,

अभिरामस्त्रिलोकानां रामः श्रीमान्स नः प्रभुः ॥ १६ ॥

abhirāmas trilok ānāṁ rāmaḥ śrī mānsa naḥ prabhuḥ . 16 .

Trans:

He—who is the destroyer of every obstacle—who is, as it were, a grove of wish-yielding trees—who is the praise of all the three worlds—He Shrī Rāma—is our Bhagwān, Lord-God Supreme.

तरुणौ रूपसम्पन्नौ सुकुमारौ महाबलौ ।

taruṇau rūpa sampannau su kumārau mahā balau ,

पुण्डरीकविशालाक्षौ चीरकृष्णाजिनाम्बरौ ॥ १७ ॥

puṇḍarīka viśāl ākṣau cīra kṛṣṇā jinām barau . 17 .

फलमूलाशिनौ दान्तौ तापसौ ब्रह्मचारिणौ ।

phala mūl āśinau dāntau tāpasau brahma cāriṇau ,

पुत्रौ दशरथस्यैतौ भ्रातरौ रामलक्ष्मणौ ॥ १८ ॥

putrau daśa ratha syaitau bhrā tarau rāma lakṣmaṇau . 18 .

शरण्यौ सर्वसत्त्वानां श्रेष्ठौ सर्वधनुष्मताम् ।

śaraṇ yau sarva satt vānāṁ śre ṣṭhau sarva dhanuṣ matām ,

रक्षः कुलनिहन्तारौ त्रायेतां नो रघूत्तमौ ॥ १९ ॥

rakṣaḥ kulani hantārau trā yetāṁ no raghū ttamau . 19 .

Trans:

Full of beauty, charming youths mighty and strong, with lotus-like broad exquisite eyes, who have donned the bark of tree and dark deer skins, who subsist on fruits and roots, who live as celibates practicing penance, those sons of Dashrath—the two brothers Rāma and Lakshman—the foremost amongst all archers, the destroyers of whole race of demons, who give life and shelter to all beings—those best of scions of Raghus, may they grant protection to me.

आत्तसज्जधनुषाविषुस्पृशावक्षयाशुगनिषङ्गसङ्गनौ ।

ātta sajja dhanuṣā viṣu spṛśā vakṣay āśuga niṣaṅga saṅganau ,

रक्षणाय मम रामलक्ष्मणावग्रतः पथि सदैव गच्छताम् ॥ २० ॥

rakṣ aṇāya mama rāma lakṣmaṇ āvagrataḥ pathi sadaiva gacch atām . 20 .

Trans:

Accompanying me, with bows pulled and ready, with their hand stroking the arrows, with quivers full of unfailing arms slung on their back—may those wayfarers Rāma and Lakshman always stay in the front—as I traverse my path—granting their protective care.

संनद्धः कवची खड्गी चापबाणधरो युवा ।
saṁ naddhaḥ kavacī khaḍgī cāpa bāṇa dharo yuvā ,
गच्छन्मनोरथान्नश्च रामः पातु सलक्ष्मणः ॥ २१ ॥
gacchan manorath ānnaśca rāmaḥ pātu sa lakṣmaṇaḥ . 21 .

Trans:

Always prepared and armored—armed with bows, arrows, swords—of youthful forms—may Rāma and Lakshman always abide ahead of me, protecting my cherished thoughts.

रामो दाशरथिः शूरो लक्ष्मणानुचरो बली ।
rāmo dāśarathiḥ śūro lakṣman ānucaro balī ,
काकुत्स्थः पुरुषः पूर्णः कौसल्येयो रघूत्तमः ॥ २२ ॥
kākuts thaḥ puruṣaḥ pūrṇaḥ kausal yeyo raghū ttamaḥ . 22 .
वेदान्तवेद्यो यज्ञेशः पुराणपुरुषोत्तमः ।
vedānta vedyo yajñ eśaḥ purāṇa puruṣ ottamaḥ ,
जानकीवल्लभः श्रीमान् अप्रमेय पराक्रमः ॥ २३ ॥
jānakī vallabh aḥ śrī mān a prameya parā kramaḥ . 23 .
इत्येतानि जपन्नित्यं मद्भक्तः श्रद्धयान्वितः ।
itye tāni japan nityaṁ mad bhaktaḥ śraddha yānvitaḥ ,
अश्वमेधाधिकं पुण्यं सम्प्राप्नोति न संशयः ॥ २४ ॥
aśva medhā dhikaṁ puṇyaṁ sam prāp noti na saṁś ayaḥ . 24 .

Trans:

Rāma, Dāsharathī [Dasharath's son], Shūro [Brave], Lakshman-anucharo [whom Lakshman follows], Balī [Powerful], Kākutstha [Kakutstha's Descendent], Purusha [the Supreme-Reality beyond Māyā], Pūrna [Complete], Kausalyeyo [Kausalyā's son], Raghūttama [Best of Raghus], Vedānta-Vedyo [Import of Vedanta], Yagyesha [Lord of Yagya], Purāṇa [Ancient-Most], Purushottama [Supreme-Most], Jānakī-Vallabha [Sītā's Beloved], Shrīmān [Lord of Prosperity], Aprameya-Parākrami [Immeasurably-Brave]—they who recites these names of Rāma everyday with faith, such devotees of mine will assuredly get the fruit of Ashwamegha Yagya and more—of this let there be no doubt [says Lord Shankar].

रामं दुर्वादलश्यामं पद्माक्षं पीतवाससम् ।
rāmaṁ durvā dala śyāmaṁ padm ākṣaṁ pīta vāsa sam ,
स्तुवन्ति नामभिर्दिव्यैर्न ते संसारिणो नराः ॥ २५ ॥
stu vanti nāmabhir div yairna te saṁ sāriṇo narāḥ . 25 .

Trans:

Chanting these divine names and singing the praises of Shrī Rāma—He, who wears yellow raiments, the lotus-eyed Lord of dark complexion, of a swarthy hue as the leaves of dark *Doorba*—the faithful are never anymore trapped in the cycle of transmigration.

रामं लक्ष्मणपूर्वजं रघुवरं सीतापतिं सुन्दरं
rāmaṁ lakṣmaṇa pūrvajaṁ raghu varaṁ sītā patiṁ sundaraṁ
काकुत्स्थं करुणार्णवं गुणनिधिं विप्रप्रियं धार्मिकम् ।
kākut sthaṁ karuṇār ṇavaṁ guṇa nidhiṁ vipra priyaṁ dhārmikam ,
राजेन्द्रं सत्यसंधं दशरथतनयं श्यामलं शान्तमूर्तिं
rājendraṁ satya saṁdhaṁ daśaratha tanayaṁ śyāmalaṁ śānta mūrtiṁ
वन्दे लोकाभिरामं रघुकुलतिलकं राघवं रावणारिम् ॥ २६ ॥
vande lok ābhirāmaṁ raghu kula tilakaṁ rāghavaṁ rāvaṇā rim . 26 .

Trans:

Unto Rāma—the revered of Lakshman, the best of the House of Raghus, the most-charming Lord of Sītā, the ocean of compassion, the scion of Kakustha, a treasurehouse of virtues, the darling of the virtuous, most religious and wise, the Sovereign King of Kings, conjoined to Truth, the dark-complexioned son of Dashrath, Embodied-Bliss, the most exquisite in creation, the crown jewel of Raghus, slayer of the demon Rāvan—unto Him, Lord Rāghav, my repeated salutations.

रामाय रामभद्राय रामचन्द्राय वेधसे ।
rāmāya rāma bhadrāya rāma candrāya vedhase ,
रघुनाथाय नाथाय सीतायाः पतये नमः ॥ २७ ॥
raghu nāthāya nāthāya sītāyāḥ pataye namaḥ . 27 .

Trans:

I bow to Rāma; my obeisance to Rāmabhadra; my many venerations to Rāmachandra, the omniscient Lord-God Raghunāth; again and again my repeated salutations to Sītāpatī—the Lord of Sītā.

श्रीराम राम रघुनन्दन राम राम
śrīrāma rāma raghu nandana rāma rāma
श्रीराम राम भरताग्रज राम राम ।
śrīrāma rāma bharat āgraja rāma rāma ,
श्रीराम राम रणकर्कश राम राम
śrīrāma rāma raṇa karkaśa rāma rāma
श्रीराम राम शरणं भव राम राम ॥ २८ ॥
śrīrāma rāma śaraṇaṁ bhava rāma rāma . 28 .

Trans:

I stand in surrender to Shrī Rāma—Rāma, Rāma, Raghunandan [Raghu Scion] Rāma. I give myself unto Shrī Rāma—Rāma, Rāma, Bharatāgraja [Bharat's Elder] Rāma. I lay my life before Shrī Rāma—Rāma, Rāma, Rankarkasha [Terrible in Battle] Rāma. I take shelter in you O Rāma—Shrī Rāma, Rāma, Rāma; be my refuge, Lord-God.

श्रीरामचन्द्रचरणौ मनसा स्मरामि
śrī rāma candra caraṇau manasā smarāmi
श्रीरामचन्द्रचरणौ वचसा गृणामि ।
śrī rāma candra caraṇau vacasā gṛṇāmi ,
श्रीरामचन्द्रचरणौ शिरसा नमामि
śrī rāma candra caraṇau śirasā namāmi
श्रीरामचन्द्रचरणौ शरणं प्रपद्ये ॥ २९ ॥
śrī rāma candra caraṇau śaraṇaṁ prapadye . 29 .

Trans:

With my heart I reverence the feet of Shrī Rāmachandra. With my speech I make veneration to the holy feet of Shrī Rāmachandra. With my head I salute the sacred feet of Shrī Rāma. Bowing low I take complete refuge at the holy feet of Rāma—who's a cooling moon to the burning worldly flames.

माता रामो मत्पिता रामचन्द्रः
mātā rāmo mat pitā rāma candraḥ
स्वामी रामो मत्सखा रामचन्द्रः ।
svāmī rāmo mat sakhā rāma candraḥ ,
सर्वस्वं मे रामचन्द्रो दयालु
sarva svaṁ me rāma candro dayālu

नान्यं जाने नैव जाने न जाने ॥ ३० ॥

rnā nyaṁ jāne naiva jāne na jāne . 30 .

Trans:

Rāma is my loving mother, and Rāma my protective father. Rāma is my gracious Lord, and Rāma my beloved friend. My everyone and everything is only Rāmachandra, the most-compassionate Lord. Other than Rāma I know of no other—absolutely, I know of no one except Shrī Rāma.

दक्षिणे लक्ष्मणो यस्य वामे च जनकात्मजा ।

dakṣiṇe lakṣmaṇo yasya vāme ca janak ātmajā ,

पुरतो मारुतिर्यस्य तं वन्दे रघुनन्दनम् ॥ ३१ ॥

purato mārutir yasya taṁ vande raghu nandanam . 31 .

Trans:

Who has Lakshmana to his right, and the daughter of Janaka to his left; before whom Hanumān is bowing down in reverence—to that Lord Raghu-Nandan I make my obeisance.

लोकाभिरामं रणरङ्गधीरं

lokā bhirāmaṁ raṇa raṅga dhīraṁ

राजीवनेत्रं रघुवंशनाथम् ।

rājīva netraṁ raghu vaṁśa nātham ,

कारुण्यरूपं करुणाकरं तं

kāruṇy arūpaṁ karuṇā karaṁ taṁ

श्रीरामचन्द्रं शरणं प्रपद्ये ॥ ३२ ॥

śrī rāma candraṁ śaraṇaṁ pra padye . 32 .

Trans:

The cynosure of eyes of all beings, the most valiant in battle, the lotus-eyed Lord of the Raghu-Lineage, the embodiment of compassion—unto that Lord-God Rāmachandra, in complete surrender I approach.

मनोजवं मारुततुल्यवेगं

mano javaṁ māruta tulya vegaṁ

जितेन्द्रियं बुद्धिमतां वरिष्ठम् ।

jit endriyaṁ buddhi matāṁ vari ṣṭham ,

वातात्मजं वानरयूथमुख्यं

vāt ātmajaṁ vānara yūtha mukhyaṁ

श्रीरामदूतं शरणं प्रपद्ये ॥ ३३ ॥

śrī rāma dūtaṁ śaraṇaṁ pra padye . 33 .

Trans:

Who is quick as the mind and equal to his sire (the Wind) in speed—unto him—who is the master of his senses and the foremost amongst the wise, unto him—the Son-of-Wind, the chief of monkey hosts—unto that messenger of Lord Rāma—Shrī Hanumān, I come seeking refuge.

कूजन्तं रामरामेति मधुरं मधुराक्षरम् ।

kū jantaṁ rāma rāmeti madhuraṁ madhu rākṣaram ,

आरुह्य कविताशाखां वन्दे वाल्मीकिकोकिलम् ॥ ३४ ॥

āruhya kavitā śākhāṁ vande vālmīki kokilam . 34 .

Trans:

He—who sports in the woods of the glories of Sītā-Rāma, like a *koel*: ever singing the sweet name of Rāma sitting on the branches of poesy—to him, the grand sage Vālmiki, I offer my salutations.

आपदामपहर्तारं दातारं सर्वसम्पदाम् ।
āpadā mapa hartāraṁ dātā raṁ sarva sampadām ,
लोकाभिरामं श्रीरामं भूयो भूयो नमाम्यहम् ॥ ३५ ॥
lokā bhirāmaṁ śrī rāmaṁ bhūyo bhūyo namām yaham . 35 .

Trans:

Unto Shrī Rāma—who takes away all perils and difficulties, who is the bestower of all prosperities and prayers, who is the most beloved of all beings in the world—I bow; and I bow repeatedly.

भर्जनं भवबीजानामर्जनं सुखसम्पदाम् ।
bhar janaṁ bhava bījā nāmar janaṁ sukha sam padām ,
तर्जनं यमदूतानां रामरामेति गर्जनम् ॥ ३६ ॥
tar janaṁ yama dūtā nāṁ rāma rāmeti gar janam . 36 .

Trans:

The chants of the name of Rāma is the fiery thunder that destructs the seed of cycle of transmigration; it is the bestower of all felicity and wealth; and it puts fear into the heart of the messenger-of-death.

रामो राजमणिः सदा विजयते रामं रमेशं भजे
rāmo rāja maṇiḥ sadā vijayate rāmaṁ rameśaṁ bhaje
रामेणाभिहता निशाचरचमू रामाय तस्मै नमः ।
rāmeṇ ābhihatā niśā cara camū rāmāya tasmai namaḥ ,
रामान्नास्ति परायणं परतरं रामस्य दासोऽस्म्यहं
rāmān nāsti parā yaṇaṁ parataraṁ rāmasya dāso 'smyahaṁ
रामे चित्तलयः सदा भवतु मे भो राम मामुद्धर ॥ ३७ ॥
rāme citta layaḥ sadā bhavatu me bho rāma mām uddhara . 37 .

Trans:

Rāma, the Crest-Jewel of Monarchs, is ever victorious. I sing the praises of Shrī Rāma, Lord of all beings. He Rāma, who decimated the whole army of night-roving demons, Him I devoutly revere. There is no greater refuge than Rāma; I am a servant of Shrī Rāma. My mind remains ever absorbed in Rāma. O Rāma Lord-God, please redeem me.

राम रामेति रामेति रमे रामे मनोरमे ।
rāma rāmeti rāmeti rame rāme mano rame ,
सहस्रनाम तत्तुल्यं रामनाम वरानने ॥ ३८ ॥
sahasra nāma tat tulyaṁ rāma nāma varā nane . 38 .

Trans:

Rāma, Rāma, Rāma—chanting this beautiful Name Rāma, my mind remains ever absorbed in God. The one name 'Rāma' is equivalent to a thousand other names of God, O fair-faced [Umā—says Shiva].

॥ इति श्रीबुधकौशिकमुनिविरचितं श्रीरामरक्षास्तोत्रं सम्पूर्णम् ॥

. iti śrī-budha-kauśika-muni-viraci-taṁ śrī-rāma-rakṣā-stotraṁ sam-pūrṇam .
— Thus ends the Rāmrakshāstotra composed by Shrī Buddha-Kaushik Muni —

(Author of this Original Sanskrit Hymn is: Buddha-Kaushik Muni [Pre-historic Sage]. Translator: Sushma)

www.ingramcontent.com/pod-product-compliance
Lightning Source LLC
Chambersburg PA
CBHW080026130526
44591CB00037B/2679
* 9 7 8 1 9 4 5 7 3 9 1 8 7 *